Easy Oracle Jumpstart
Oracle Database Management Concepts and Administration

Steve Karam
Robert G. Freeman

As this is my first published book, you may find my dedication a little long. However, I owe a debt of gratitude to many people for their influence in my career, and so I feel it necessary to extend my thanks.

I would like to partially dedicate this book to Jim Bagley, Randolf Julian, Dan Gaertner and all the other DBAs of Dominion Enterprises who learned with me the true meaning of long hours and late nights.

I also want to thank Joe Fuller for instilling in me the critical sense of urgency, and Chad Gray, the fastest programmer I've ever known.

I want to extend a special dedication to my family: my mom for allowing me to call her bluff, my dad for his wisdom and encouragement, my step-dad for teaching me to be steadfast, my sister Stephanie for forcing me to learn to think on my feet, and my other siblings Courtney, Trevor, Samantha, and Ryan for their love and support. And special thanks to my aunt and godmother Concetta for giving me my first computer when I was 8 years old; I wouldn't have gotten to this point if it were not for her.

Most importantly, I'd like to thank my wife, Kristina, for adding love, joy, and beauty to my life and inspiring me to be the best I can be.

Steve Karam

Easy Oracle Jumpstart
Oracle Database Management Concepts and Administration

By Steve Karam and Robert G. Freeman

Copyright © 2006 by Rampant TechPress. All rights reserved.

Printed in the United States of America.

Easy Oracle Series Book #4

Published by: Rampant TechPress, Kittrell, NC, USA

Editors: John Lavender, Janet Burleson, and Robin Haden

Production Editor: Teri Wade

Production Manager: Janet Burleson

Cover Design: Janet Burleson

Illustrations: Mike Reed

Printing History: January 2007 for First Edition

ISBN: 0-9759135-5-7

ISBN-13: 978-0-9759135-5-0

Library of Congress Control Number: 2005901264

Table of Contents

The Easy Oracle Series 1

Conventions used in this Book 3

Acknowledgements 5

Chapter 1: Inside the Oracle Architecture **7**

Introducing Databases and Oracle 7

    Oracle can be flexible and simple too! *8*

    Oracle and the Computer *9*

    Oracle automation makes Oracle Simple *11*

The Physical Oracle Architecture 12

    Diving into the RAM Pools *14*

    Oracle Background Processes *22*

    Database Files *27*

    The Instance and the Database *30*

The Oracle Architecture 31

    Oracle Tablespaces *32*

    Blocks *33*

    Extents *33*

    Segments *34*

    Logical Oracle Structures - The Big Picture *34*

Conclusion 36

Chapter 2: Installing Oracle and Creating a Database **38**

Installing and Creating Oracle Databases 38

    The Install Guide *38*

    Checking the Edition and Version of Oracle *39*

    Choosing Oracle Features *39*

    Extra-cost Oracle Options *41*

    Checking for Compatibility Issues *43*

    Disk space allocation *43*

    Using the Oracle Universal Installer *44*

    Installed Components *49*

The Database Creation Assistant (DBCA) 50

Starting the DBCA.. *50*
Deciding What Kind of Database to Create.............................. *52*
Additional Database Configuration.. *54*
Configuring the Flash Recovery Area....................................... *57*
Create the Sample Schemas.. *58*
Configuring Memory Usage... *58*
Database Storage Settings... *60*
Finishing the Database Creation.. *62*
Connecting to the Database 64
Connecting to the Database with the SQL*Plus Client.......... *65*
The SQL*Plus Command Line Interface *67*
Putting SQL*Plus to Work.. *69*
Conclusion... 70

Chapter 3: Basic Oracle Database Administration **71**
Database Documentation 71
Books of Interest *72*
Starting and Stopping the Database 72
The Startup Command... *73*
The instance shutdown command... *78*
Inside the Oracle Data Dictionary 81
The Oracle initialization parameter file 82
Introducing the PFILE and SPFILE *83*
Administering Oracle Redo Logs 90
Administer the Archived Redo Logs.. *94*
Administering Oracle UNDO.. *100*
Administering Tablespaces.. *102*
Conclusion.. 108

Chapter 4: Administering Oracle Objects and Constraints ...**109**
Administering Oracle Objects and Constraints 109
Administering Oracle Tables.. 110
Oracle Tables.. *110*
Creating Tables.. *111*
Altering Tables.. *116*
Dropping Tables.. *118*

Inside the Oracle Data Dictionary 119
Tables and Statistics 120
   How to Generate Statistics.. *122*
   Gathering System Statistics, Data Dictionary Statistics, and Fixed
   Statistics *124*
Administering Oracle Indexes.. 129
   Creating Indexes *133*
   Altering Indexes *134*
   Dropping Indexes.. *135*
   Special Non-Tree Indexes *135*
   Oracle index dictionary views.. *140*
   Generating Indexes on Statistics *141*
Administering Oracle Views... 141
   Inside Oracle Views.. *141*
   Benefits of Oracle Views *142*
   The downside to using Views... *144*
Administering Oracle Constraints 144
   Check Constraints *145*
   NOT NULL Constraints.. *146*
   PRIMARY KEY Constraints *146*
   UNIQUE Constraints *147*
   FOREIGN KEY Constraints *147*
Conclusion.. 150

Chapter 5: Oracle Users and Security.................................. **152**

Administration of Oracle Users.. 152
   Creating Users... *153*
   Administering Oracle Users *154*
   Dropping Users.. *155*
Oracle Users and Security 155
   System Privileges *156*
   Object Privileges *159*
   Synonyms... *160*
   Using Oracle Roles *164*
Conclusion.. 165

Chapter 6: The Oracle Data Dictionary and Dynamic Performance Views 166

The Oracle Data Dictionary 166
The Purpose of the Data Dictionary 167
The Architecture of the Data Dictionary 167
Using the Data Dictionary 170
The Dynamic Performance Views 174
The purpose of the Dynamic Performance Views 175
The architecture of the Dynamic Performance Views 175
Conclusion 182

Chapter 7: Oracle Backup and Recovery 184

Protecting Databases 184
Backup a Database with RMAN 185
Recovery of the Database with RMAN 190
Conclusion 194

Chapter 8: SQL and SQL*Plus 195

All about SQL 195
The SELECT statement 198
Conclusion 204

Chapter 9: Programming in PL/SQL 205

Introduction to PL/SQL 205
PL/SQL Basic Structure 208
IF/THEN/ELSE Statements 215
The PL/SQL WHILE Loop 217
The PL/SQL REPEAT-UNTIL Loop 218
The PL/SQL FOR Loop 219
Conclusion 221
Index 222

About Steve Karam 228

About Robert Freeman 229

About Mike Reed 230

The Easy Oracle Series

Congratulations on your purchase of Easy Oracle Jumpstart. This is the first of a five book set that is specifically designed to get you started fast with Oracle technology. These books are designed by certified Oracle experts and trainers who have years of experience explaining complex Oracle topics in plain English.

Following completion of Easy Oracle Jumpstart, you are ready to move on to the subsequent Easy Oracle books:

- *Easy Oracle SQL and SQL*Plus* – Get started fast writing Oracle queries.

- *Easy Oracle PL/SQL Programming* – A proven step-by-step approach to programming with Oracle PL/SQL.

- *Easy Oracle Automation* – Learn about the automation features of Oracle.

- *Easy Oracle PHP* – Learn how to create powerful web applications using the Oracle database.

- *Free Oracle 10g Reference Poster* – Just do a Google search for "free Oracle poster" to get your free copy of the Oracle reference poster.

These books are priced right to help you get started fast in Oracle technology.

www.rampant.cc

Are you WISE?

Get the premier Oracle tuning tool. The Workload Interface Statistical Engine for Oracle provides unparallel capability for time-series Oracle tuning, unavailable nowhere else.

WISE supplements Oracle Enterprise Manager and it can quickly plot and spot performance signatures to allow you to see hidden trends, fast.

WISE interfaces with STATSPACK or AWR to provide unprecedented proactive tuning insights. Best of all, it is only $9.95. Get WISE download Now!

www.wise-oracle.com

Got Scripts?

This is the complete Oracle script collection from Mike Ault and Donald Burleson, the world's best Oracle DBA's.

Packed with over 600 ready-to-use Oracle scripts, this is the definitive collection. It would take many years to develop these scripts from scratch, making this download the best value in the Oracle industry.

It's only $49.95 (less than 7 cents per script!). For immediate download go to:

www.oracle-script.com

Conventions used in this Book

It is critical for any technical publication to follow rigorous standards and employ consistent punctuation conventions to make the text easy to read.

However, this is not an easy task. Within Oracle there are many types of notation that can confuse a reader. Some Oracle utilities such as STATSPACK and TKPROF are always spelled in CAPITAL letters, while Oracle parameters and procedures have varying naming conventions in the Oracle documentation. It is also important to remember that many Oracle commands are case sensitive, and are always left in their original executable form, and never altered with italics or capitalization.

Parameters - All Oracle parameters will be lowercase italics. Exceptions to this rule are parameter arguments that are commonly capitalized (KEEP pool, TKPROF), these will be left in ALL CAPS.

Variables - All PL/SQL program variables and arguments will also remain in lowercase italics (*dbms_job, dbms_utility*).

Tables & dictionary objects – All data dictionary objects are referenced in *lowercase italics (dba_indexes, v$sql)*. This includes all *v$* and *x$* views (*x$kcbcbh, v$parameter*) and dictionary views (*dba_tables, user_indexes*).

Programs & Products - All products and programs that are known to the author are capitalized according to the vendor specifications (IBM, DBXray, etc). All names known by Rampant TechPress to be trademark names appear in this text as initial caps. References to UNIX are always made in uppercase.

Learn More – Look for this icon to find more information about a specific topic. A Google search string will follow it that will take you to supplemental information from the Burleson Consulting sites. An example would be, **bc oracle concepts documentation**.

Acknowledgements

This type of highly technical reference book requires the dedicated efforts of many people. Even though we are the authors, our work ends when we deliver the content. After each chapter is delivered, several Oracle DBAs carefully review and correct the technical content. After the technical review, experienced copy editors polish the grammar and syntax.

The finished work is then reviewed as page proofs are turned over to the production manager, who arranges the creation of the online code depot, if needed, and manages the cover art, printing distribution, and warehousing.

In short, the authors play a small role in the development of this book, and we need to thank and acknowledge everyone who helped bring this book to fruition:

Janet Burleson, for the production management, including the creation of the cover art, page proofing, printing, and distribution.

Teri Wade, for her help in the production of the page proofs.

John Garmany, for donating the content for the chapter on SQL and PL/SQL.

Thanks to all the people at Rampant who were involved in the process of completing this book. It could never have happened this way without you.

Many thanks,

Steve Karam

Inside the Oracle Architecture

"Why does Oracle have to be SO HARD?"

Introducing Databases and Oracle

At a high–level, Oracle can be thought of as nothing more than a large electronic filing cabinet, or a place to store and retrieve information. At the computer level, Oracle is a computer program that manages an electronic filing cabinet.

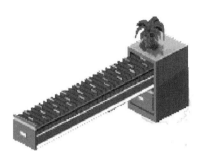

One reason that Oracle has become a world dominant database is because it runs on just about every platform imaginable, from a mainframe to a Macintosh.

Today, most shops run Oracle in UNIX, Linux, and Windows.

Oracle runs on almost every computer ever made, with over 60 diverse platforms such as Intel, Sun Solaris, IBM mainframes, and many, many others.

Today, Oracle is considered the world's most powerful, flexible and robust database. Along with this power comes complexity.

Oracle can be flexible and simple too!

Oracle has become the world's most flexible database and it stores much more than text and numbers. An Oracle database supports video, audio and complex spatial applications that are used to build jet fighters and submarines.

Unlike simpler databases, every aspect of Oracle's behavior can be controlled. A DBA can control how rows are placed on the data blocks and how Oracle performs hundreds of resource management issues.

However, Oracle can be simple too! In Oracle 10g, artificial intelligence tools provide basic management, making Oracle a very simple database. The savvy DBA can choose to make the Oracle database simple or robust.

If databases were people, Oracle might look like this, especially when compared to the other less powerful data storage programs:

Oracle   *Other Databases*

As with all software, Oracle must interface with the computer it is installed on in order to utilize its hardware. Oracle is extremely knowledgeable about how to partake of individual processor power, RAM, and other resources. This will be covered in the next section.

Oracle and the Computer

Oracle has an optimization for every environment, and teams of experts make sure that Oracle takes advantage of every possible system component, including the following:

- System processors.
- System Memory.
- The network.
- Disk Storage.

Oracle uses all of these components to store data and make it available to users who have a right to use it. Each of these components can influence Oracle database performance. Slow components can make for a slow database; fast components can make for a fast database.

Oracle is for professionals, not dilettantes and neophytes

At a high-level, Oracle is a large computer program. When this Oracle program starts, it will grab the following from the computer:

- **RAM memory** – Oracle allocates a chunk of RAM memory, called the System Global Area (SGA).

- **Programs** – Oracle launches about a dozen slave programs called background processes.

- **Disk** – Oracle creates files on disk drives for everything from the database transactions to the tables that are created and populated. From the moment a database is created, Oracle allocates .dbf files onto disk.

In sum, Oracle takes control over the computer, based on the initialization parameters provided. These parameters will be covered in subsequent chapters.

Oracle can take control over your computer

Remember, even though Oracle is complex and has many components, it is still just a big computer program. Don't get scared by big words or concepts; anyone can use Oracle.

Note! This chapter will introduce a number of new terms. Because of the nature of Oracle, it is likely that terms will be used in this chapter that have not been completely introduced yet. Just hang tight; if a new term is used, it will probably be explained in more detail later

Oracle automation makes Oracle Simple

In order to make the world's most robust and complex database easy to use for beginners, Oracle has added automation features to control the internal complexity.

Starting in Oracle 10g, Oracle has used artificial intelligence to automate many of the DBA tasks.

Oracle has automated the computer hardware, performing almost all storage management, CPU and RAM management.

Oracle also helps tune Structured Query Language (SQL) queries and has intelligent advisors. The automated areas include Automated Memory Management (AMM), Automated Storage Management (ASM) and Automatic Database Diagnostic Management (ADDM). To learn the details, the book *Easy Oracle Automation* by Dr. Arun Kumar is highly recommended. It is the next book in the Easy Oracle series and a great follow-up to this book.

⚏ Type the following string into the Google search engine to find more information: **oracle easy automation book**

The following section will provide an overview of Oracle's physical architecture.

The Physical Oracle Architecture

Where people work, and where they live, all have an architecture that keeps the building together. This architecture, if well designed, will keep the building from falling apart, keep occupants nice and warm, provide a nice parking place and will provide easy access to facilities like water fountains and restrooms. A well -crafted architecture will help people work more efficiently. The same is true for databases.

Despite the name Oracle, there is no magic!

The architecture around which Oracle has built its database is designed to perform quickly, efficiently, and without errors.

In this section, the Oracle architecture will be introduced. This architecture includes the following components:

- The System Global Area (SGA) and other memory areas that utilize RAM

- Database related background processes

- Tablespaces and Datafiles

- Database related files

- The instance and the database

The next step will be to look at each of these components in more detail. Finally, the components will be assembled into a single big picture view, to show how all these pieces fit together to complete the Oracle puzzle. The information in this chapter is limited to the overall database architecture. Later chapters will delve into the finer details of managing these structures.

The next section will drill down a bit deeper into the architecture of Oracle and explore memory structures, which are the part of Oracle that utilizes the computer system's RAM.

Diving into the RAM Pools

All computers have memory. Memory should not be confused with disk storage. Memory is volatile, which means its content is lost after the power is removed. Memory is also very fast. RAM memory is expressed in nanoseconds or billionths of a second, and disk speed is in milliseconds or thousandths of a second. Needless to say, RAM speed is much faster than disks.

⚏ Type the following string into the Google search engine to find more information: **oracle cache disk speed**.

Don't get burned by tiny pools

Disk storage is non-volatile. This means that the data stored on a disk will remain after the power is turned off. Disks are always slower than RAM, but disks are hundreds of times cheaper than RAM.

There is a trade-off between memory and disks: Memory is fast but expensive, usually about $1,000 per gigabyte, whereas disks are slower but very cheap. Thus, memory is used for short-term storage of information that is frequently needed and disks are used for long-term storage of information.

Oracle has a number of memory areas that it uses to store information. The following sections will address the main Oracle memory areas. They are called:

- **The System Global Area** (SGA) – RAM areas for the Oracle programs.

- **The Program Global Area (PGA)** – Private RAM areas for individual client connections to Oracle

The SGA will be covered first.

The SGA RAM Region

The System Global Area (SGA) is a group of shared memory areas that are dedicated to an Oracle instance. The database programs and RAM are considered an instance.

All Oracle processes use the SGA to hold information. The SGA is used to store incoming data and internal control information that is needed by the database. The amount of memory to be allocated to the SGA is controlled by setting Oracle initialization parameters. These might include *db_cache_size, shared_pool_size* and *log_buffer*. The data buffers are defined by the *db_cache_size* parameter.

In Oracle Database 10g only two parameters need to be configured to define the SGA. They are the *sga_target* and *sga_max_size*. If these parameters are configured, Oracle will calculate how much memory to allocate to the different areas of the SGA using a feature called Automatic Memory Management (AMM). More experienced DBAs may want to manually allocate memory to each individual area of the SGA with the initialization parameters.

Type the following string into the Google search engine to find more information: **oracle amm**.

The SGA was sub-divided into several memory structures and each has a different mission. The main areas of interest contained in the SGA have complicated names, but are actually quite simple:

- *db_cache_size* – the buffer cache

- *shared_pool_size* – the shared pool

- *log_buffer* – the redo log buffer

These memory areas will be covered in more detail in the following sections.

Inside the Data Buffer Cache

The Buffer Cache or database buffer cache is where Oracle stores data blocks. With few exceptions, any data coming in or going out of the database will pass through the buffer cache.

The total space in the Database Buffer Cache is sub-divided by Oracle into units of storage called blocks. Blocks are the smallest unit of storage in Oracle and the data file blocksize can be controlled when the database files are allocated.

An Oracle block is different from a disk block. An Oracle block is a logical construct, a creation of Oracle, rather than the internal block size of the operating system. In other words, Oracle is provided with a big whiteboard and it takes pens and draws a bunch of boxes on the board that are all the same size. The whiteboard is the memory, and the boxes that Oracle creates are individual blocks in the memory.

Each block inside a file is determined by the *db_block_size* parameter and the size of the default blocks is defined when the database is created. The size of the default database block size is user defined. Tablespaces can also be defined with different block sizes. For example, many Oracle professionals place indexes in a 32k block size and leave the data files in a 16k block size.

⊟ Type the following string into the Google search engine to find more information: **oracle multiple blocksizes**.

When Oracle receives a request to retrieve data, it will first check the internal memory structures to see if the data is already in the buffer. This practice allows to server to avoid unnecessary I/O. In an ideal world, DBAs would be able to create one buffer for each database page, thereby ensuring that Oracle Server would read each block only once.

The *db_cache_size* and *shared_pool_size* parameters define most of the size of the in-memory region that Oracle consumes on startup and determine the amount of storage available to cache data blocks, SQL, and stored procedures.

🖳 Type the following string into the Google search engine to find more information: **oracle sga size**.

The default size for the buffer pool (64k) is too small. It is suggested that this be set to a value of 1m when Oracle is configured.

Inside the Shared Pool

The Oracle shared pool contains Oracle's library cache, which is responsible for collecting, parsing, interpreting, and executing all of the SQL statements that go against the Oracle database. Hence, the shared pool is a key component, so it's necessary for the Oracle database administrator to check for shared pool contention.

The shared pool is like a buffer for SQL statements. Oracle's parsing algorithm ensures that identical SQL statements do not have to be parsed each time they are executed. The shared pool is used to store SQL statements, and it includes the following components:

- The library cache

- The dictionary cache

- Control structures

The following table lists the different areas stored in the shared pool and their purpose:

SHARED POOL AREA	DESCRIPTION
Shared SQL Area	The shared SQL area stores each SQL statement executed in the database. This area allows SQL execution plans to be reused by many users.
Private SQL Area	Private SQL areas are non-shared memory areas assigned to unique user sessions.
PL/SQL Area	Used to hold parsed and compiled PL/SQL program units, allowing the execution plans to be shared by many users.
Control Structures	Common control structure information, for example, lock information.

Table 1.1: *Library Cache Components*

The *dictionary cache* stores metadata which is data about the tables and indexes. It is also known as the row cache. It is used to cache data dictionary related information in RAM for quick access. The dictionary cache is like the buffer cache, except it's for Oracle data dictionary information instead of user information. The data dictionary will be covered later in this book.

As with the database buffer cache, the shared pool is critical to performance. The concept of Oracle SQL statement reuse will be explored later in this book. Reusability is a concept that is very important when it comes to performance relating to the shared pool!

⛁ Type the following string into the Google search engine to find more information: **oracle sql caching**.

This section covered Oracle's in-memory storage of data, SQL, and control structures but there is one other very important SGA structure to be examined, the redo log buffer.

The Redo Log Buffer

The redo log buffer is a RAM area that is defined by the initialization parameter *log_buffer*. It works to save changes to data in case something fails and Oracle has to rollback the data, or put it back into its original state. Data Manipulation Language (DML) is the process by which Oracle SQL updates a table. During this process, redo images are created and stored in the redo log buffer. Since RAM is faster than disk, this makes the storage of redo very fast.

Oracle will eventually flush the redo log buffer to disk. This can happen in a number of special cases, but what's really important is that Oracle guarantees that the redo log buffer will be flushed to disk after a commit operation occurs. When changes are made in the database they must be committed to make them permanent and visible to other users.

Oracle commit Processing

A COMMIT is a very important Oracle concept. As users make changes in Oracle, those changes are only visible to the user session making the change and are unrecoverable in the case of a crash. A COMMIT changes all that. When the user tells Oracle to commit the change, Oracle makes the change visible to everyone, and ensures that the change is recoverable.

Since RAM is wiped out if power to the computer is lost, all the redo data in the redo buffer would be lost in a power outage. To protect against this problem, a COMMIT asks Oracle to save the redo to disk, which is permanent. The redo log disk files are called online redo logs.

Inside the PGA

Not all RAM in Oracle is shared memory. When a user process is started it has a private RAM area which is used for sorting SQL results and managing special joins called hash joins. This private RAM is known as the Program Global Area (PGA). Each

---

individual PGA memory area is allocated each time a new user connects to the database.

🖧 Type the following string into the Google search engine to find more information: **oracle pga sizing**.

Oracle Database 10g will manage the PGA if the *pga_aggregate_target* parameter is set. The topic of parameters and how they are set is covered later in this book. The size of the PGA can be manually allocated via parameters such as *sort_area_size* and *hash_area_size*. Most experts recommend that Oracle be allowed to configure these areas. It is acceptable to manually configure the *pga_aggregate_target* parameter.

The PGA can be critical to performance, particularly if the application is doing a large number of sorts. Sort operations occur if the ORDER by and GROUP BY commands are utilized in SQL statements.

The Big Picture – The Oracle Instance

Now that information has been presented on Oracle RAM regions, it is a good time to take a look at the big picture. Below is a graphic that shows all of the different memory areas within the SGA. This graphic shows the server processes that are created for each user connection.

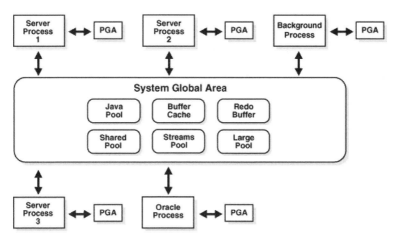

Figure 1.1: *Oracle Memory Areas*

Oracle Background Processes

Although Oracle can conceptually be viewed as a large computer program, in reality Oracle is a collection of many programs called background processes. Each program is assigned to a specific job. The Oracle database can have a lot of processes running, depending on how the database is configured. There are two different kinds of background processes associated with Oracle, required processes and optional processes. These will be covered in more detail next.

Oracle Database Required Processes

Here are some of the most important Oracle background processes:

- **SMON** - System Monitor process recovers after instance failure and monitors temporary segments and extents. SMON, in a non-failed instance, can also perform failed instance recovery for a failed instance.

- **PMON** - Process Monitor process recovers failed process resources. If MTS, also called Shared Server Architecture, is

---

being utilized, PMON monitors and restarts any failed dispatcher or server processes.

- **DBWR** - Database Writer or Dirty Buffer Writer process is responsible for writing dirty buffers from the database block cache to the database data files. Generally, DBWR only writes blocks back to the data files on commit, or when the cache is full and space has to be made for more blocks.

- **LGWR** - Log Writer process is responsible for writing the log buffers out to the redo logs.

- **ARCH** – The optional Archive process writes filled redo logs to the archive log location(s).

⚏ Type the following string into the Google search engine to find more information: **oracle background processes**.

The Log Writer Process

The redo log buffer was presented earlier in this chapter along with information on how its contents are transferred to disk regularly. The Log Writer Process (LGWR) is responsible for the movement of this redo.

Like all the other slave programs, the LGWR process is started when the database is started, and it is shutdown when the database is shutdown. On regular intervals, LGWR will move the redo from the redo log buffer to online redo log files, which are files designed to store the redo. The online redo logs will be covered in more detail later in this chapter.

The Database Writer Process

The Database Writer (DBWR) process is responsible for writing data from the RAM buffer cache to the database datafiles on disk. The database datafiles are physical files on disk, *customer.dbf* for example. The default is to have one database writer process, but large databases can have multiple DBWR processes.

The Checkpoint Process

The Checkpoint Process is responsible for updating file headers in the database datafiles. A checkpoint occurs when Oracle moves new or updated blocks, called dirty blocks, from the RAM buffer cache to the database datafiles. A checkpoint keeps the database buffer cache and the database datafiles synchronized. This synchronization is part of the mechanism that Oracle uses to ensure that the database can always be recovered.

The Process Monitor Process

The Process Monitor is the janitor of the database, cleaning up trash left over from aborted user sessions. An example would be when a client abnormally disconnects from the database. If this should happen, it is the job of the Process Monitor (PMON) process to cleanup after that failure. PMON will cleanup memory areas and other database resources that were in use by that user process. PMON constantly checks the status of user and database processes. In some cases, failed database processes can be restarted by PMON.

The System Monitor Process

When Oracle database is stated, Oracle will perform several checks to see if the database is healthy.

SMON manages your database for you!

If Oracle finds a problem at startup time, the System Monitor process (SMON) will perform recovery activities. SMON also performs certain types of database maintenance. These activities occur in the background and have no real impact on normal database operations.

Optional Oracle Background Processes

The Oracle database comes with a number of additional processes that are optional.

For example, Oracle comes with a program that allows the user to schedule the times that certain database programs will run. This program is known as the job scheduler process. The job scheduler is an optional program that must be enabled for it to operate.

When the job scheduler is enabled, a process or program will be started to control the job scheduler. This is known as the Job Queue Process. Here are the most common optional processes:

PROCESS NAME	DESCRIPTION
Job Queue Process (CJQ)	Used for the job scheduler. The job scheduler includes a main program (the coordinator) and slave programs that the coordinator executes. The parameter *job_queue_processes* controls how many parallel job scheduler jobs can be executed at one time.
Archiver Process (ARCn)	Used to archive online redo logs, which are covered later in this chapter, to disk. In cases when it is needed, Oracle Database 10g will start the *ARCn* process automatically. If additional ARCn processes are needed, then the Oracle Database will start up to 9 additional processes.
Queue Monitor Process (QMNn)	Used to manage Oracle Streams Advanced Queueing.
MMON, MMNL, MMAN	Used to perform various database management tasks.

Table 1.2: *Optional Oracle Database Processes*

Now that information on the basic Oracle background processes has been presented, it is a good time to look at how they all interface. The picture below shows that the SGA is the main point of contact between processes, providing shared RAM storage:

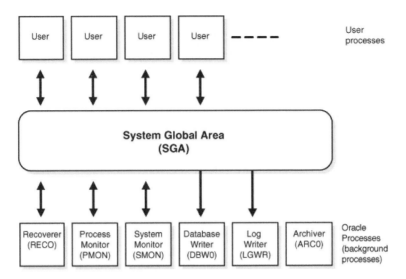

Figure 1.2: *Oracle Processes*

The final topic related to architecture will involve looking at the data files where the information is stored.

Database Files

The final components of the Oracle architecture are the physical files where information resides on disk. Oracle has several types for data files, each serves a different purpose:

- Database datafiles
- Control files
- Online redo logs
- Parameter files
- Other database related files

Each of these physical files will be explored in a bit more detail.

Database datafiles

Database datafiles are physical files stored on disk. These files are used to store data on disk. With a few exceptions, database datafiles are only written to by the DBWR processes that were introduced earlier.

These database datafiles are associated with Oracle tablespaces, which are logical containers for tables and indexes.

Control files

The Control File of the database is a binary file that contains a great deal of database information. The control file contains the database name and data about the database log files. Oracle cannot function without valid control files. If the control file is not available, the database will not start. If a control file is lost while the database is running, the database will crash.

Type the following string into the Google search engine to find more information: **oracle control file errors**.

Because the control file is so important, Oracle allows duplicate copies of the control file to be maintained. When there is more than one control file, the user is said to be multiplexing the control files. It is a good practice to put these multiple copies on different disks to protect the control file. Later in this book, this duplication will be illustrated.

Online redo logs

Think of the online redo logs like a tape recorder that records every change in the Oracle database. As changes occur, they are regularly recorded in the online redo logs, just like a movie is recorded on a VCR.

In the event that a disk crashes, it may be necessary to replace the disk and restore the disk data from a backup tape. If this backup tape was several days ago, lots of data has been lost.

Fortunately, Oracle can replay the saved transactions in the online redo logs and re-apply lost transactions back into the database. Many times, this means that Oracle can recover from a crash without the DBA having to do anything other than just telling the database to startup. The topic of online redo log files and how they relate to database recovery will be covered in later chapters of this book.

At a minimum, Oracle requires that there be two online redo logs assigned to the database. Oracle will write redo to the first log, and when the first log is full, Oracle will switch to the second log and write the same redo. Each of these individual online redo logs is known as an online redo log group.

The reason they are called groups is that there can be mirrored copies of the online redo log files in each group. Like control files, it's a good idea to have multiplexed copies of the Online redo logs. Oracle allows the user to define multiple copies of these files. Each copy is called a member. Each redo log group can have one or more members.

Parameter file

The parameter file, sometimes called *init.ora*, contains configuration information for the database to use at startup time. The parameter file configures how much RAM the database is going to use, where to find the control files, where to write trace files, and a whole host of other information. In most cases the database will not start without a parameter file. Oracle allows there to be a manual parameter file called a PFILE or a server-side parameter file called an SPFILE.

⚏ Type the following string into the Google search engine to find more information: **bc oracle parameters**.

Other Database Related Files

When working with the Oracle database users will be introduced to a number of different kinds of files. The following table is a list of the most common files and their general purpose. As this book progresses, many of these files will be introduced in more detail.

PROCESS NAME	DESCRIPTION
Oracle Trace Files	Created by Oracle in a number of different situations. These can be created as a result of a database crash, a session failure, an unexpected but non-fatal database failure, or based on specific user operational commands.
Alert log	This is the general log file for each Oracle database.
Networking configuration files	These files are used to configure the different network components of the Oracle database. These include files such as *tnsnames.ora* and *listener.ora*.
Oracle Database Software Binaries	The Oracle Database software includes the basic programs that allow the database to function.

Table 1.3: *Other Oracle Database Files*

The Instance and the Database

This is almost the end of the introduction to the Oracle database architecture. This journey cannot be completed until two additional terms are defined, instance and database. The Oracle instance is the combination of the Oracle SGA and the related background processes, the programs, PMON, SMON, etc. When the SGA RAM memory is successfully allocated and the Oracle database processes are running normally, the instance is said to be up.

However, and instance is sometimes different from a database. An instance can be running, but the database might not be mounted or open. The Oracle Database includes the physical files that have been covered: the datafiles, the control file, and the redo log files. When the Oracle instance is running, it can attach itself to a database, mount the control file, and finally open the datafiles and redo log files. This is an important distinction because many Oracle operations must be done with the instance started while the database is not open.

The Oracle Architecture

In the previous section, the Oracle physical architecture was presented. Things like files, programs, and hardware are all considered physical pieces or physical properties of the Oracle database. This section will focus on the logical pieces of the Oracle database.

Oracle segregates physical components such as the .dbf files on disk, by mapping them into logical containers called tablespaces. In turn, tables and indexes are allocated inside these tablespaces and Oracle takes care of the interface to the physical disk files.

This section will focus on the following logical database elements:

- Tablespaces, which are actually not completely logical

- Blocks

- Extents

- Segments

A big-picture summary will be presented of the relationships between these logical objects. This section just provides some basic concepts. Much more detail will follow in the chapters to come!

Oracle Tablespaces

Tablespaces are the bridge between certain physical and logical components of the Oracle database. Tablespaces are where Oracle database objects, such as tables, indexes, and rollback segments are stored. A tablespace can be thought of like a shared disk drive in Windows. A user can store files on a shared drive, move files around, and remove files. The same is true with tablespaces.

A tablespace is made up of one or more database datafiles. The total amount of storage space available in a tablespace is the sum of the physical disk size of all the datafiles associated with that tablespace, less some system overhead. The datafiles are created automatically when the tablespace is defined. In most cases, all datafile space is pre-allocated; that is, the space is set aside when the datafile is created. Thus, when a tablespace is created, the initial size of the associated datafile is defined. The specifics of creating tablespaces will be presented later in this book.

Tablespaces are given names as they are created. For example, the first tablespaces that are created are named SYSTEM and SYSAUX, though SYSAUX is only created in 10g.

⊞ Type the following string into the Google search engine to find more information: **oracle tablespace scripts**.

Tablespaces are generally named based on the objects within the tablespace. For example a tablespace might be named PAYROLL_DATA if it is going to store payroll related information. Tablespaces will be presented in greater detail in later chapters in this book.

Blocks

A block is the smallest unit of storage in Oracle. The size of a database block is fixed when the database is created, and cannot be changed except by rebuilding the database from scratch. The database block size is fixed at 2K, 4K, 8K, 16K, or 32K in size. Once the base block size is defined, new tablespaces can be created with alternate block sizes.

The Oracle instance also includes a RAM buffer cache which is made up of RAM blocks which map to the data block in the physical datafiles.

Extents

An *extent* is an uninterrupted or contiguous allocation of blocks within a segment. Extents are assigned to a segment automatically by Oracle. A user will rarely deal directly with an extent, rather they will deal directly with its associated segment.

⟳ Type the following string into the Google search engine to find more information: **bc oracle extents**.

An extent must be on contiguous blocks within a single datafile, so an extent cannot span multiple Oracle datafiles. Oracle will allocate the size of the extents based on the type of tablespace. Extent allocation will be presented in later chapters when table and index creation are covered.

Segments

Segments are the storage objects within the Oracle database. A segment might be a table, an index, a cluster, or any one of more than 20 object types.

The DBA creates the segments and assigns them to a specific tablespace. In most cases a single segment cannot reside in more than one tablespace. However, a segment can be split up or partitioned into different tablespaces.

When a segment is created, its initial size is defined. The creation of segments in Oracle will be covered in much more detail in chapters to come.

Logical Oracle Structures - The Big Picture

The following figure shows the relationship between segments, extents, and blocks in the database. In this example, a single segment has been created. This segment actually consists of two extents. Each of the two extents consists of a number of contiguous blocks.

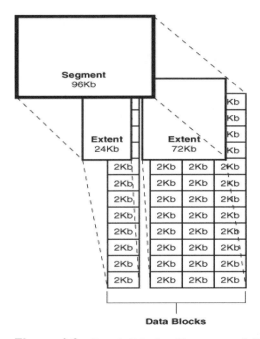

Figure 1.3: *Oracle Blocks, Extents and Segments*

This concludes Chapter One and it is time to see a complete map of an Oracle database.

Do not worry if everything is not clear yet. Proceeding through the next chapters, and actually working with the database, will help all this make much better sense!

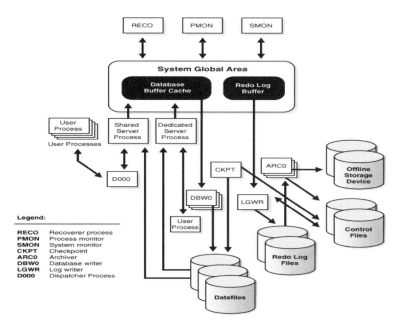

Figure 1.3: *Oracle Blocks, Extents and Segments*

This Figure depicts a RAM region, the system global area, interacting with Oracle's programs, CKPT and ARC0. It also depicts how Oracle programs read and write data to the disk files.

Type the following string into the Google search engine to find more information: **bc oracle background**.

Conclusion

The main points of this chapter include:

- Oracle is the world' most powerful, flexible, and robust database.

- Oracle is very complex.

- Oracle 10g administration can be simplified with automation features.

- The configuration of Oracle is governed by initialization parameters, called *init.ora.*

- An Oracle instance consists of a RAM memory region called the SGA, plus a set of Oracle programs called background processes.

The next chapter takes a look at how to create and install an Oracle database.

Installing Oracle and Creating a Database

This chapter will cover how the Oracle database software is installed, and then the method for creating an Oracle database will be introduced. After the Oracle database has been created, the SQL*Plus interface to the Oracle database will be explored.

Installing and Creating Oracle Databases

Before an Oracle database can be created, the database software must first be installed. The software for Oracle Database 10g comes on only one CD, so installation is easy. This section will cover what needs to be done before the Oracle software is installed. Once that is accomplished, the installation of the Oracle software can be completed.

Before the Oracle software is installed, make sure the right edition and version of Oracle are being utilized.

The Install Guide

There is a separate install guide for each hardware platform and it's critical to that this manual be read before trying to install Oracle.

Frequently basic questions appear in forums where it is clear the person asking the question has not read the installation guide. It is rumored that the DBA guild is considering doubling its rates for any emergency calls to fix install disasters, so read up folks! It is time to get started.

Checking the Edition and Version of Oracle

When preparing to install the Oracle software for the first time, it is necessary to determine the desired release and features. When considering what version of Oracle to use, consider the following issues:

- **Features** - Different versions of the Oracle database software have different functionality. Versions in Oracle are numbered, like 9.2.0.6 or 10.1.0.3, and they indicate the release level of the software. Go to Oracle's web site, www.oracle.com, to find out what features are available in the various versions of Oracle.

- **Edition** - Oracle version is one consideration, but in each version there are editions that come with different functionality. Make sure that the required features are available in the chosen edition of Oracle. The names change with each release, but Oracle Database 10g comes in Enterprise Edition, Standard Edition and Personal Edition. Advanced functionality is missing from Standard Edition (SE) and Express Edition (XE).

- **Version** - Make sure that the version being installed is still supported by Oracle, and that it will not soon be de-supported. It can be very time consuming, and sometimes expensive, to migrate to different versions of Oracle.

Choosing Oracle Features

Many companies that choose to forgo the advanced features of the Enterprise Edition may save thousands of dollars per year in licensing fees. The features available in Oracle Enterprise Edition that are not available in Oracle Standard Edition (SE), Oracle Express (XE), or Standard Edition One (SEO) include many features that may not be required:

- **Advanced Replication** - This tool provides one-way and multi-master replication, via database links, for distributed systems using the *dbms_repcat* package.

- **Transparent Application Failover (TAF)** - Used to re-direct in-flight transactions to a failover database when a server crash occurs.

- **Fast-start fault recovery** - This is a method for quick recovery and synchronization of the Oracle database when hardware failures occur.

- **Oracle Data Guard** – Data Guard is a semi-automated standby/failover database for database replication.

- **Advanced Queuing** - A software scheduling package for serialization using the *dbms_aqadm* package.

- **SQL Optimizer Plan Stability (Stored Outlines)** - This is a tool to freeze Oracle execution plans during software upgrades and change vendor SQL when the source SQL cannot be touched.

- **Online index rebuilds** - The ability to rebuild an Oracle index while it is being updated.

- **Export transportable tablespaces** - This provides the ability to transfer encapsulated tablespaces between databases.

- **Materialized Views** - This is a powerful tool to allow for the pre-summarization of aggregate data (averages, counts, sums) and pre-joins tables together. Materialized views are especially useful in low-update databases and data warehouses.

- **Bitmap indexes** - Bitmaps are a unique indexing structure for fast combinations of low-cardinality data columns. Bitmap indexes are especially powerful for data warehouses and low-update databases.

- **Oracle Parallel Query (OPQ)** - Parallel query is a divide and conquer approach whereby Symmetric Multiprocessing (SMP) and Massively Parallel Processors (MPP) can get super-fast response time for large-table full-table scans

- **Parallel DML** - This is the ability to perform database changes (inserts, updates, deletes) in parallel.

- **Parallel index rebuilding** - This allows large Oracle indexes to be rebuilt in a fraction of the time required by a single CPU system.

- **Parallel index scans** - This feature allows for parallel fast full-index scans and multi-block reads of index data blocks.

- **Parallel backup & recovery** - This allows Oracle RMAN backups to be parallelized for super-fast backups of large databases.

- **Incremental backup & recovery** - This feature tracks database changes and only backs up those components that have been changed since the last backup.

- **Oracle connection manager (CMAN)** - Thos tool is used for Oracle databases that must support large volumes of concurrent user connections.

- **Oracle Streams** - Oracle offers many different methods for database failover and replication.

Extra-cost Oracle Options

In addition, Oracle offers many extra-cost database features that can be purchased independently from the edition. These include:

- **Oracle Partitioning Option** - Oracle divide-and-conquer approach for super-large databases. Partitioning is generally used for databases over 100 gigabytes.

- **Oracle Real Application Clusters (RAC)** - RAC is the Oracle flagship software for scalability and high availability. Free with Oracle Standard Edition and licensed at an extra cost with Enterprise Edition. RAC is an integral part of Oracle10g Grid computing. Oracle RAC is an extra-cost option for systems that require continuous availability and super-high scalability.

- **Oracle OLAP** - Oracle is a leader in data warehouse technology and has Online Analytical Processing (OLAP) tools for advanced decision support and multi-terabyte data warehouses.

- **Oracle Data Mining** - Advanced data warehouse systems require tools to locate hidden trends and correlations. Oracle offers a tool with advanced artificial intelligence for finding hidden data correlations in super-large databases.

- **Oracle Database Diagnostic Pack** - This covers access to the Oracle10g Automated Workload Repository (AWR) and Automatic Database Diagnostic Monitor (ADDM) components.

- **Oracle advanced Security** - Oracle advanced Security provides sophisticated security control for confidential and secure data systems.

- **Oracle Tuning Pack** - Oracle provides a full suite of online tools for tuning the Oracle database. Integrated with the Oracle Enterprise Manager, Oracle tuning pack competes with many 3rd-party vendor tuning products.

- **Oracle Change Management Pack** - The change management pack provides complete version control and database change auditing.

Type the following string into the Google search engine to find more information: **bc oracle license features**.

The next step is to verify compatibility issues.

Checking for Compatibility Issues

Before Oracle is installed, computer hardware and operating system compatibility should be confirmed. It is important to make sure that all of the pieces of the system work together, and that is what checking compatibility is all about. The following things need to be checked:

- **OS Version -** The version of the operating system

- **Hardware -** The hardware platform on which the system is being run. Most releases of Oracle require at least 512k in RAM.

- **OS Patches -** Required patches, including OS patches and hardware firmware patches as required.

- **Compatibility** - The compatibility of applications with the chosen combinations of hardware, OS, and Oracle version.

Oracle database compatibility information is available from the Oracle web site (www.oracle.com). When Oracle Database 10g is installed, the installer will insure that the system is configured properly, but it may abort if something is missed.

Disk space allocation

The base Oracle footprint takes a little over two gigabytes of disk space. If other optional products are going to be used, users must also check the documentation for those products for their space requirements. Usually, when planning disk space for the Oracle installation, users will want to have lots of extra space for any patches that might need to be downloaded. Patches can easily be as big as the initial install.

At least 5 gigabytes of free disk space is recommended. This makes the process of migrating to newer versions of Oracle much easier. In addition, there are plenty of logs that will end up in the installation location. Most Oracle professionals reserve at least 5 to 10 Gigabytes for the base Oracle installation.

Using the Oracle Universal Installer

The Oracle installer is called the Oracle Universal Installer (OUI). Written in Java, OUI has the same look-and-feel on any of Oracle's 60+ supported platforms. One of the nice features of Oracle Database 10g is that the installer only needs to use one CD. In previous versions there were up to 3 different CD's. Of course, additional CD's are required to load optional products.

The Oracle Database software can also be downloaded from Oracle Corporation's web site at www.oracle.com.

🖳 Type the following string into the Google search engine to find more information: **oracle downloads**.

The download is free for non-commercial use. However a license will have to be purchased to use it for purposes other than learning.

To start the Oracle installer on a Windows environment, simply put the Oracle Database 10g CD in the CDROM drive and the autorun will start the installer. If autorun is disabled, simply double click setup from the CD.

For other platforms, follow the directions in the platform-specific install instructions:

- Mounting the CD

- Changing to the CD mount point. Do not do this if 9i is being installed or the CD will not eject on Linux or UNIX platforms.

- Running the installer. In UNIX this is typically called runInstaller.

The Oracle installer makes the install process quite easy. Simply follow the prompts. The following section steps through a typical installation.

 Tip: To run the Oracle Installer on UNIX, make sure an X-Windows session can be started on the console being used. In order for the Oracle Installer to function properly, the user must be able to run X.

Installing the Oracle Software

Once the installer is started, the first screen that appears is the Welcome screen:

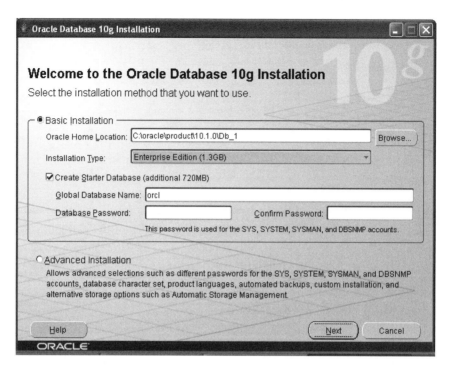

Figure 2.1: *Oracle Installer Welcome Screen*

This example will walk through a typical install without creating the starter database. Because of this, the Create Starter Database box needs to be un-checked.

If the install needs to run Oracle on another disk drive, enter the new location in the box titled Oracle Home Location. Now, press the Next button.

At this point, Oracle will collect information about the server environment. For example, occasional errors may be generated that say that Oracle can not determine an IP address. This is typical in a Windows environment where there is a dynamic IP address. To avoid this, create a temporary entry in the *hosts* file with the current static IP address of the server.

Once the installer has collected external information it will present a summary screen of all the products that may be installed.

Figure 2.2: *Oracle Installer Summary screen*

At this point, click the Install button and Oracle will begin to install the database software. A progress bar will track the progress of the installation.

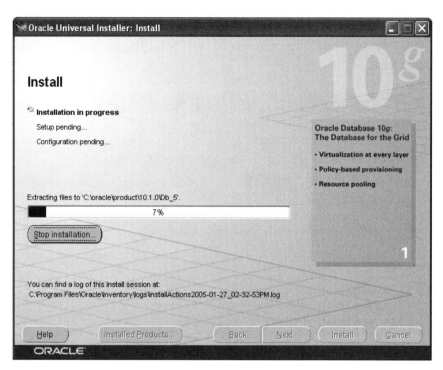

Figure 2.3: *Installation Progress*

The install may take up to ten minutes, so just be patient as it loads and links the executables. The install can be stopped by clicking on the Stop installation button.

Once the install is complete, the following screen will be displayed:

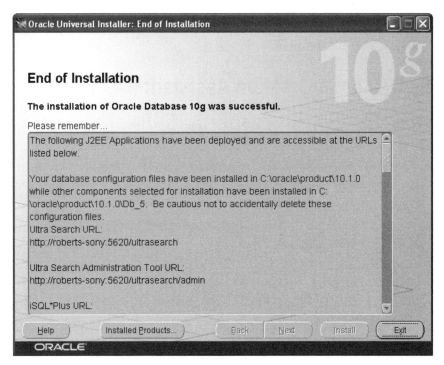

Figure 2.4: *Oracle Installer successful installation screen*

This screen provides a lot of information, and the Ultra Search URL and the iSQL*Plus URL should be noted. When the End of Installation screen appears, the install is complete and the installer can be exited by clicking the Exit button.

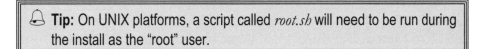
> **Tip:** On UNIX platforms, a script called *root.sh* will need to be run during the install as the "root" user.

Installed Components

The Oracle software is placed in a location called ORACLE_HOME. In the example given here, the ORACLE_HOME was created in a directory named c:\oracle\product\10.1.0\Db_5.

Now it is time to create a database.

The Database Creation Assistant (DBCA)

While a database can be created manually, the beginning DBA is really better off letting Oracle handle the internals. The Database Creation Assistant (DBCA) wizard guides the user through the database creation process. This section will demonstrate creating a database using the DBCA.

Starting the DBCA

To start the DBCA from the Windows desktop choose Start → Oracle OraDB10g_Home1, or whatever the Oracle Home location was named → Configuration and Migration Tools → Database Configuration Assistant.

 If using Linux or UNIX, the DBCA can be opened from the command prompt with the simple command *dbca*. However, previous to doing this, certain environment variables may have to be set up:

$ export ORACLE_HOME=your_installation_directory
$ export PATH=$PATH:$ORACLE_HOME/bin
$ dbca

The Oracle Database Configuration Assistant (DBCA) will start once this selection is made and the DBCA welcome screen will be displayed:

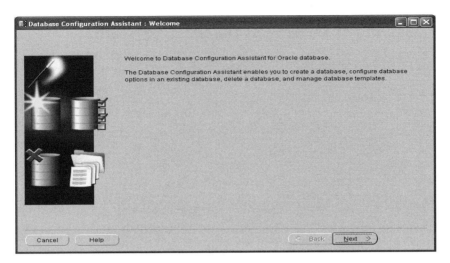

Figure 2.5: *DBCA Welcome Screen*

Simply press the Next key to continue the database creation. Here is the first screen:

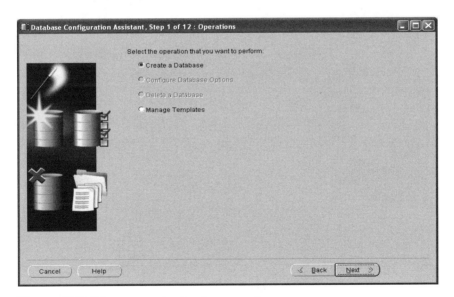

Figure 2.6: *First screen in database creation process*

Deciding What Kind of Database to Create

Notice that the DBCA can perform several functions:

- Creation of a database
- Configuration of database options
- Removal of a database
- Management of database templates.

For the purposes of this chapter, creation of a database will be examined. Since this option is highlighted already, just click on the Next button. The screen that appears next prompts for the type of database to create.

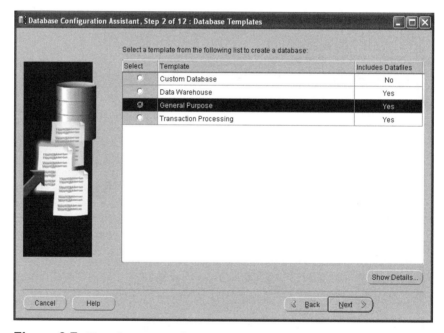

Figure 2.7: *Database type selection*

Again, Oracle provides a number of options:

- Creation of a custom database without a template.

- Creation of a data warehouse database from a template.

- Creation of a general purpose database from a template.

- Creation of a transaction processing database from a template.

Note: Once the user is more accustom to creating databases, the *Creation of a custom database without a template* option will likely be used the most.

In this example, a General Purpose database will be created. The data warehouse or transaction processing database creation process is much the same as the one shown here.

Creating a Custom database requires answering many more questions and is beyond the scope of this book.

Remember, the DBCA is for beginners. Once a user is more comfortable with Oracle, experimenting with the custom database creation option can be done, and eventually moving on to manual database creation.

The next screen prompts for the Global Database Name and the Database System Identifier (SID). In this example, the database will be called BOOKTST.

🔔 Tip: Naming the Oracle Database

Naming the database correctly is important. While names like Enterprise, Picard or B5 might sound cool they are not very practical. The following four to six character naming standard is recommended:

AAATT
Where: AAA = Application Identifier
       TTT = Database Type

The Application identifier defines the principal use of the database. If it was an accounting application, the letters ACT might be used for the Application Identifier.

The database type implies that there are different kinds of databases associated with a given application identifier. The most common database types are:

- Production – PRD
- Test – TST
- QA – QA
- Development – DEV

Given this example, the production accounting database would be called ACTPRD, and the test accounting database would be called ACTTST.

Additional Database Configuration

Now that the ORACLE_SID has been chosen, press Next to proceed:

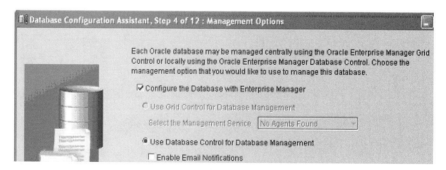

Figure 2.8: *Oracle Enterprise Manager Screen*

This window allows the configuration of the Oracle Enterprise Manager (OEM). It also allows the enablement of OEM options for automated backups and email notifications. For purposes of this example, these options will not be configured. Simply click on the Next button to proceed.

The next window is very important. It allows passwords to be set on DBA level accounts, such as SYS and SYSTEM:

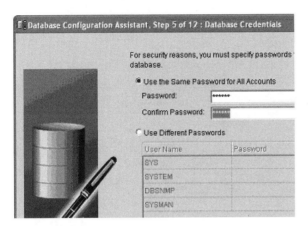

Figure 2.9: *Specify passwords for DBA level accounts*

All accounts can have a common password or specific passwords can be configured for each account. For this example, all accounts will be set to use the same password. The common password for this example is *shadow*. Hence, enter *shadow* in the password and confirm password boxes, and click Next. The next step is to choose the file system type:

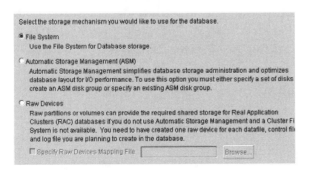

Figure 2.10: *Selecting the file system type*

For this example, the default will be used. If a RAC cluster is being created, or if ASM or Raw file systems are being used, the other options that DBCA makes available via this screen should be explored.

Click Next to proceed. The next screen is where the storage location for database related files will be designated.

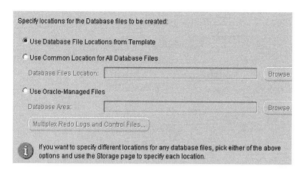

Figure 2.11: *Select where database related files will be stored*

As DBA's become more experienced, they will learn that file placement can make a big difference in database performance. In this example, Oracle will be allowed to determine the location of the datafiles. Click Next to proceed.

Configuring the Flash Recovery Area

The next screen allows the configuration of the Oracle flash recovery area. This is a new feature in Oracle Database 10g, and will be covered later in this book. The flash recovery area is very important because it is where Oracle stores a number of important backup and recovery files. Here is an example of the Recovery Options screen:

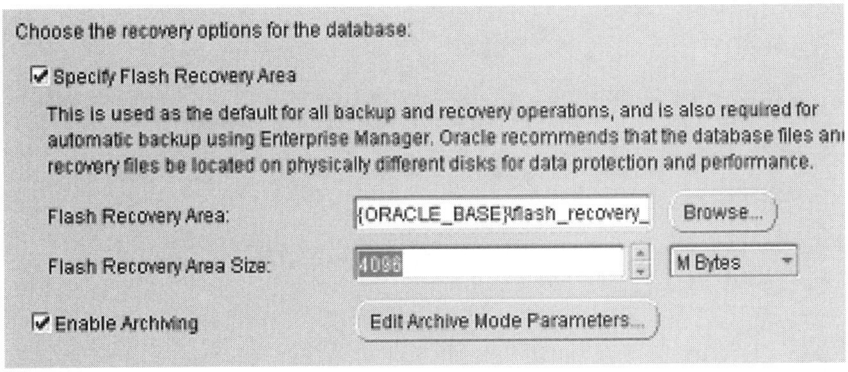

Figure 2.12: *Recovery Options Screen*

For this example, the two default values have been changed. First, the size of the Flash Recovery Area has been doubled. This value defaults to 2 Gigabytes (2GB), which is frequently is too small. Second, the Enable Archiving checkbox has been selected. This setting will tell Oracle to configure the database in ARCHIVELOG mode and Oracle will use the redo logging mechanism that was covered in Chapter One.

The ARCHIVELOG mode also makes Oracle database backup and recovery much easier. It is strongly recommended that any production Oracle database be in ARCHIVELOG mode. ARCHIVELOG mode will be covered in more detail later in this book. Having made the two suggested changes, click Next to continue.

Create the Sample Schemas

The next screen that is displayed is the Sample Schemas screen:

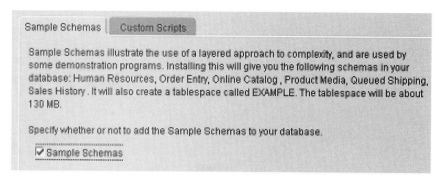

Figure 2.13: *Sample Schemas screen*

By selecting the Sample Schemas option, Oracle will create several small sample schemas that can use for practice.

As users learn Oracle and practice with Oracle-supplied examples, these sample schemas will come in handy. Click Next to continue the database creation.

Configuring Memory Usage

The next screen is Memory specification, a very important part of the install:

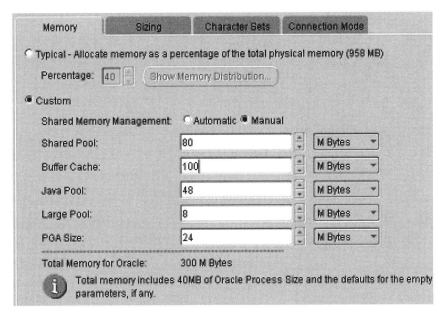

Figure 2.14: *Memory Allocation screen*

This screen allows modification of the initialization parameters for memory pools such as *db_cache_size*, and *shared_pool_size*. The database block sizes need to be set the character set for the database chosen. In this example, the buffer cache was increased to 100 megabytes.

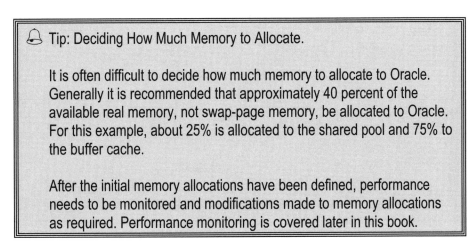

🔔 Tip: Deciding How Much Memory to Allocate.

It is often difficult to decide how much memory to allocate to Oracle. Generally it is recommended that approximately 40 percent of the available real memory, not swap-page memory, be allocated to Oracle. For this example, about 25% is allocated to the shared pool and 75% to the buffer cache.

After the initial memory allocations have been defined, performance needs to be monitored and modifications made to memory allocations as required. Performance monitoring is covered later in this book.

If Oracle is being installed on a PC, remember that a 32-bit PC can only allocate about 1,700 megabytes (1.7 GB). The SGA should also be kept small, under 1,500 megabytes. Here are some guidelines for allocating memory:

- **Over-allocation** – Making the SGA too big can cause nasty things to happen on the operating system like paging and swapping of memory out to disk. More is not always better. Only allocate as much memory as the system really needs.

- **Share the RAM** – Be careful not to take away RAM that might be used by other programs or databases on the server. On an Oracle dedicated server, a general rule of thumb is to never allocate more than about 60 to 65 percent of memory to the database. This reserves memory for other Oracle and non-Oracle processes.

Also note that the memory allocation screen allows modification to the SGA pool sizes, such and the Java pool and the all-important PGA. After all changes are made, click Next to continue.

Database Storage Settings

The next screen allows changes to be made to database storage parameters:

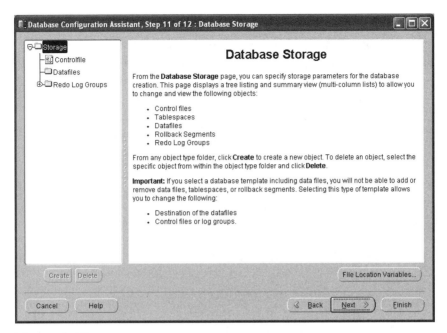

Figure 2.15: *Database Storage Parameters*

This screen allows tablespaces to be added or removed, the size of the datafiles that are associated with those tablespaces to be adjusted, modification to the online redo logs, etc. In this example, the default is acceptable, so click Next to continue.

It is almost time to create a database!

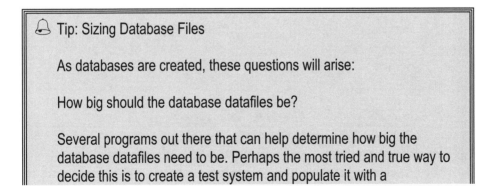

🔔 Tip: Sizing Database Files

As databases are created, these questions will arise:

How big should the database datafiles be?

Several programs out there that can help determine how big the database datafiles need to be. Perhaps the most tried and true way to decide this is to create a test system and populate it with a representative set of data, say one or two percent of the size of production. Once this is done, simply extrapolate from there how big the production database will need to be. Hence, if the test database is 10MB with one percent of the data, the production database will be 1000 MB.

How big should the database Online Redo Logs be?

After creating the database, monitor how often the online redo logs switch, on average. The online redo logs should be sized such that they switch no more frequently than every 15 minutes.

Finishing the Database Creation

There is one more screen to go before Oracle can create a database. In this last screen Oracle displays two different options with regard to the actions that DBCA should take. The first option allows the creation of a template for the new database. The second option actually instructs Oracle to create the database. Here is an example of this screen:

Figure 2.16: *Database Creation Options screen*

In this example, Oracle will create a database and will not save these settings as a database template. Click on Finish, and the

DBCA will present a summary of all of the database creation actions that it will take.

Press OK when that window appears and Oracle will start the creation of the database. A screen will be displayed that shows the progress of the database creation process.

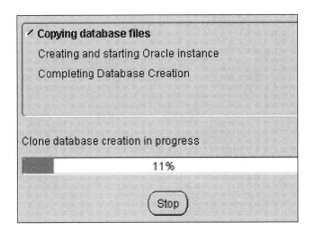

Figure 2.17: *Database creation progress*

The following screen will be presented when Oracle has completed creating the database. Depending on the speed of the system, it could take several minutes.

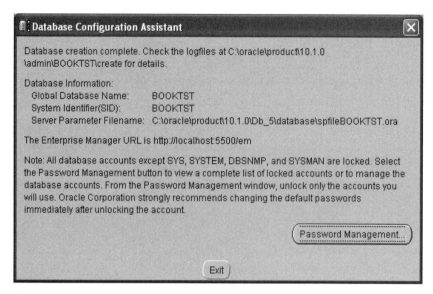

Figure 2.18: *Database Creation Complete*

This screen provides the opportunity to view and modify any accounts that were created by the DBCA. In this example, there is no need to modify any of the accounts. Click the Exit button. Congratulations, a database has been created! Now it is time to connect to the database for the first time!

Connecting to the Database

There are a number of ways to log into the newly created Oracle database. Programmers will use things like ODBC, JDBC and OCI to connect to a database from their applications. DBA's have a number of tools available to them that allow them to connect to and manage databases including SQL*Plus and Oracle Enterprise Manager (OEM). Also, a number of third party tools are available for use that can help manage Oracle databases.

Connecting to the Database with the SQL*Plus Client

This section will cover the principle DBA interface into Oracle, SQL*Plus. There are two versions of SQL*Plus readily available. The first is the SQL*Plus client version which can be installed on any Windows based PC.

To start the SQL*Plus client from Windows click on Start → *Your_oracle_home_location* → Application Development → SQL Plus. The SQL*Plus login screen appears.

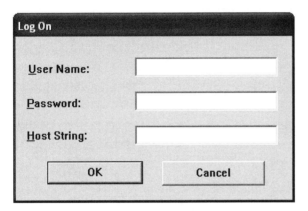

Figure 2.19: *SQL*Plus Login Screen*

A database has been created using DBCA and a password was assigned to the DBA management account. Now it is time to login as SYS. To do so, type the following entries:

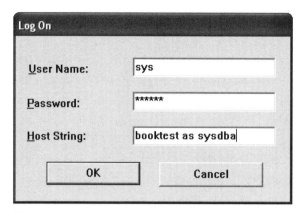

Figure 2.20: *SQL*Plus Login Screen with entries*

In this example, the connection is being made to the SYS account of the database that was just created. The SYS account is an all powerful account in Oracle, and it should never be used lightly.

Notice the host string setting. Here the database name, booktest, is entered and the command as sysdba has been added. Most non-DBA's will never use the as sysdba command, for it implies special privileges are granted to the person logging in. In this example, as the DBA, these special privileges are needed.

At this point, the user is logged into Oracle, and SQL*Plus is ready to accept commands. Additionally, there is another version of SQL*Plus out there called iSQL*Plus. It has an Internet interface.

This figure shows what the SQL*Plus client looks like once it comes up:

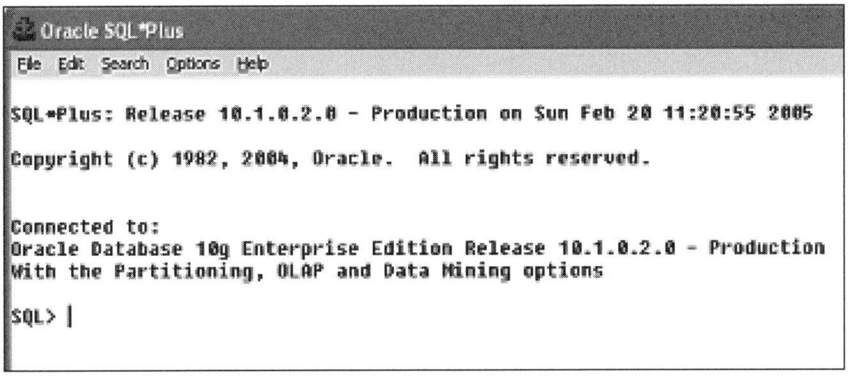

Figure 2.21: *SQL*Plus client screen after login*

The SQL*Plus Command Line Interface

SQL*Plus also comes with a command line interface. To start SQL*Plus at the command line, following these instructions:

- If connecting to a local database, the *oracle_sid* environment parameter must be set to the name of the database. Here is an example of doing this in Windows, followed by an example of setting the *oracle_sid* in UNIX. The UNIX example shows setting the Oracle Home and path information as well so UNIX can find the binaries:

Windows:

```
C:>Set ORACLE_SID=booktst
```

UNIX/Linux:

```
export ORACLE_SID=booktst
export ORACLE_HOME=your_install_location
export PATH=$PATH:$ORACLE_HOME/bin
```

- Next, start SQL*Plus with the *sqlplus* command. When starting SQL plus include the user name to connect to. Here are examples of the use of this command:

```
C:\>sqlplus john_dba

SQL*Plus: Release 10.1.0.2.0 - Production on Sun Feb 20 11:28:13
2005

Copyright (c) 1982, 2004, Oracle.  All rights reserved.

Enter password:

Connected to:
Oracle Database 10g Enterprise Edition Release 10.1.0.2.0 -
Production
With the Partitioning, OLAP and Data Mining options

SQL>
```

Note in the example above that when SQL*Plus is started, the name of the user account must be provided. In this case, the account *john_dba* was used. Next, SQL*Plus will prompt for the password to this account. The password will not be visible as it is being entered. If the correct password is entered, Oracle will proceed to the SQL prompt (SQL>).

The password can also be included when SQL*Plus is called, but this means that the password will not be hidden, and this can have serious security implications. Here is an example of using the user account and the password to log into SQL*Plus:

```
/u01/app> sqlplus john_dba/my_password
```

If this is done in a UNIX/Linux environment, the command *ps – ef* will display the password for anyone to see.

To perform specific DBA activities on the database, such as backing up the database or shutting it down, it is necessary to log in as a special type of user. This is because these operations require a special set of administrative privileges called the SYSDBA and SYSOPER privileges.

To activate these privileges, the DBA's user ID must be allowed to access these privileges. How to set up this account will be covered later in this book. A special connection string must be used to connect to the database to activate these privileges. Use the following command to connect using the SYSDBA privileges. These are super DBA privileges.

```
C:\>sqlplus "sys as sysdba"
```

The password can be included if desired:

```
C:\>sqlplus "sys/my_password as sysdba"
```

The same method of connecting also works with the SYSOPER privilege. Simply replace *sysdba* with *sysoper* in the connection string. One final thing to note is that the connection string is enclosed in quotes. This is required because there is white space (blanks) inside the connection string.

Putting SQL*Plus to Work

DBA's and developers are the most common users of SQL*Plus, and database management is frequently performed from SQL*Plus. SQL stands for Structured Query Language. It is the language that is used to communicate with Oracle, and it is the language that is used in SQL*Plus. There will be lots of examples of SQL in this book, and they will be covered in detail as they are presented so do not worry about the specifics of the language just now.

The following activities are examples of the things that a DBA will do from SQL*Plus:

- Create, Drop and alter database objects
- Startup and shutdown the database
- Create, Drop and alter database users
- Manage database security

- Manage database backup and recovery operations

The SQL *Plus prompt is also used to access the data within the Oracle database. DBA's, developers, and even end-users will use SQL*Plus to execute database queries using the SQL language.

Conclusion

This has been a quick and dirty installation and setup of Oracle. While there are many more options available during the installation phase, they are things that will be utilized at a later time.

The main points of this chapter include:

- The Oracle Universal installer is the tour guide through the installation process.

- There are several steps to installing Oracle, including the loading of the executables and the creation of databases.

- Oracle provides the Database Creation Assistant (DBCA) to help create databases.

In the chapters to come, Oracle will be used in many different ways. This information will help the user begin to understand more of the advanced options that can be performed as early as the installation phase of the software.

Basic Oracle Database Administration

Now that Oracle is installed and a database has been created, it is important to examine how to manage the complete database system. In this section, the topics will include:

- Database Documentation
- Startup and Shutdown of the Database
- The Data Dictionary
- Oracle Parameter Files
- Storage structures

Database Documentation

Oracle is a large software package, formed of dozens of products and components. As such, it is well documented with literally thousands of pages of documentation.

At times, however, that much documentation is very hard to wade through. Thankfully, Oracle provides an outstanding website with all the documentation compiled at http://tahiti.oracle.com. In addition, Oracle documentation can also be searched for specific needs at http://search.oracle.com.

Oracle documentation also comes in the form of books, each written on different subjects. These books usually are divided by concepts, such as database administration, backup and recovery, or SQL command references.

With every new version of Oracle will come new documentation; however, the basic topics always remain the same.

While official documentation is great, sometimes the answer can be found just as easily via other means.

⌨ Type the following string into the Google search engine to find more information: **oracle google keywords**.

Books of Interest

Aspiring DBA's will find the following books to be the best suited for their needs:

- The SQL Reference Guide

- The Oracle Database Reference

- The Oracle Concepts Guide

- The Oracle Administrators Guide

- Oracle Backup and Recovery

Once this book has been read, these authors highly recommend the *Oracle Concepts Guide*. It contains many more concepts that are beyond the scope of this book, yet very beneficial for those wishing to master Oracle.

Starting and Stopping the Database

One of the most common jobs of the database administrator is the startup and shutdown of the Oracle database. Database shutdowns should be kept to a minimum, as it can cause unanticipated issues. Database shutdowns can:

- Cause a major inconvenience to end users

- Introduce the risk that the database will not come back up due to corruption

- Empty Oracle's memory regions, such as the database buffer cache, causing degraded performance upon start-up

However, there are times when a database shutdown is required. These times include:

- The applying of a patch or upgrade

- When application maintenance is required

- Cold backups, which require a database shutdown prior to copying the data.

- A bug in the Oracle software requiring a restart of the database

- Recovery of Oracle files in the case of a database failure

- When it is requested by support professionals to fix an issue with a database or instance.

SQL*Plus, Oracle's command line interface, is used to restart or bounce the database. This is done with simple commands that will be reviewed next.

The Startup Command

In order to start an Oracle Database, the *startup* command must be used. The command must be performed as a user with either the SYSDBA or SYSOPER privileges. For the first startup, the SYS account will be used.

```
C:\Documents and Settings\Rampant>set oracle_sid=booktst
C:\Documents and Settings\Rampant>sqlplus "sys as sysdba"

SQL*Plus: Release 10.1.0.2.0 - Production on Mon Feb 21 12:35:48

Enter password: xxxx
Connected to an idle instance.

SQL> startup
```

```
ORACLE instance started.

Total System Global Area   251658240 bytes
Fixed Size                    788368 bytes
Variable Size              145750128 bytes
Database Buffers           104857600 bytes
Redo Buffers                  262144 bytes
Database mounted.
Database opened.
```

This first example comes from a Windows XP Server. First, the *oracle_sid* environment variable is set to the name of the database that is being logged into. Second, the SQL*Plus command line tool is logged into using *sys as sysdba* as the login method.

This provides the privileges that are needed to start up the database. In this instance, a password was required to gain entry to the database. However, there may be times that logging in with SYS as SYSDBA requires no password; this is because SYSDBA is a special privilege that uses operating system authentication. User authentication will be covered in a later chapter.

The last step is issuing the *startup* command. This is all it takes to bring the database up in most cases, thereby allowing normal users to log in and interact with the database.

When Oracle is trying to open the database, it goes through three distinct stages, and each of these is listed in the startup output listed previously. These stages are:

▪ Startup (nomount)

▪ Mount

▪ Open

These stages will be explored in a bit more detail.

The Startup (nomount) Stage

When the startup command is issued, the first thing the database will do is enter the nomount stage. During the nomount stage, Oracle first opens and reads the initialization parameter file, *init.ora,* to see how the database is configured. For example, the sizes of all of the memory areas in Oracle are defined within the parameter file.

After the parameter file is accessed, the memory areas associated with the database instance are allocated. Also, during the nomount stage, the Oracle background processes are started. Together, these processes and the associated allocated memory are referred to as the Oracle instance. Once the instance has started successfully, the database is considered to be in the nomount stage. Oracle will then automatically move onto the next stage of the startup, the mount stage.

Starting the Oracle Instance (Nomount Stage)

There are some types of Oracle recovery operations that require the database to be in nomount stage. When this is the case, there is a special startup command that needs to be issued: *startup nomount.* An example is shown in this example:

```
SQL> startup nomount
```

The Mount Stage

When the startup command enters the mount stage, it opens and reads the control file. The control file is a binary file that tracks important database information, such as the location of the database datafiles.

In the mount stage, Oracle determines the location of the datafiles, but does not yet open them. Once the datafile locations have been identified, the database is ready to be opened.

Mounting the Database

Some forms of recovery require that the database be opened in mount stage. To put the database in mount stage, use the startup mount command as seen here:

```
SQL> startup mount
```

If the database instance has already been started with the startup nomount command, it can be changed from the nomount to mount startup stage using the *alter database* command:

```
SQL> alter database mount;
```

The Open Stage

The last startup step for an Oracle database is the open stage. When Oracle opens the database, it accesses all of the datafiles associated with the database. Once it has accessed the database datafiles, Oracle makes sure that all of the database datafiles are consistent.

Opening the Database

To open the database, use the *startup* command as shown in this example:

```
SQL> startup
```

If the database is mounted, it can be opened with the *alter database open* command as seen in this example:

```
SQL> alter database open;
```

Opening the Database in Restricted Mode

The database can also be started in restricted mode. Restricted mode will only allow users with special privileges to access the database, even though the database is technically open. Typically this will be DBA's. The STARTUP RESTRICT command is used to open the database in restricted mode as seen in this example:

```
SQL> startup restrict
```

The database can be switched in and out of restricted mode with the ALTER DATABASE command as seen in the following example:

```
-- Put the database in restricted session mode.
SQL> alter database enable restricted session;

-- Take the database out of restricted session mode.
SQL> alter database disable restricted session;
```

Note: Any users connected to the Oracle instance when going into restricted mode will remain connected; they must be manually disconnected from the database by exiting gracefully or by the DBA with the ALTER SYSTEM KILL SESSION command.

Problems during Oracle Startup

The typical DBA life is like that of an airline pilot, long moments of boredom followed by small moments of sheer terror. One place for sheer terror is an error during a database startup.

The most typical reason for a database not starting up is a prior database crash, data corruption, disk failure, or some other catastrophic event from which the database cannot recover. In these cases, database recovery mode is required to start the instance. There is a chapter on recovery later in this book and the topic of what to do when Oracle will not startup will be covered then.

The instance shutdown command

The database might be brought down to make configuration changes, for a backup, or to upgrade Oracle software. When it is time to bring the database down, the SHUTDOWN command is used.

The SHUTDOWN command comes in many forms. Oracle has three shutdown modes:

- **Normal** (default) - waits for in-flight work to complete

- **Immediate** - terminates all sessions and does a rollback on all uncommitted transactions

- **Abort** - aborts all sessions, leaving current DML in need of rollback, de-allocates the SGA, and terminates the background processes.

The normal and immediate modes can take a long time if there are in-flight transactions. Many Oracle DBA's ensure a swift clean shutdown this way, aborting the sessions, re-starting to allow warmstart rollback of the aborted transactions, and a shutdown immediate to close cleanly:

```
SQL> shutdown abort
SQL> startup
SQL> shutdown immediate
```

Normal Shutdown

A normal shutdown of an Oracle database is actually rarely used. This is because the normal shutdown waits for everyone to complete their work and then logoff in an orderly fashion. When a normal shutdown occurs, the database is closed in a normal manner, and all changes made in the database are flushed to the database datafiles. This is known as a clean shutdown.

Most of the time this is not practical... there always seems to be someone who has left for vacation and who forgot to log out, or there are times that Oracle processes become zombied. Zombied is when Oracle thinks someone is connected to the database but they really are not. In these cases, the database will never come down.

It will simply wait forever until those sessions are manually killed. Because of this, the SHUTDOWN IMMEDIATE or SHUTDOWN ABORT commands are often recommended. These will be covered in more detail in the next sections. Here is an example of the use of the normal shutdown command.

```
SQL> shutdown
```

When a shutdown is executed, Oracle will flush all the changes in memory out to the database datafiles. This makes database startup quicker because the database is in a consistent state.

Think of it this way: if a man jumps into the air and lands on his feet, he has landed in a way that prepares him to make another jump. If, instead, he jumps and lands on his back, he is in no position to make another jump; instead, he must perform a recovery by taking the actions required to stand again. A clean shutdown is one that is prepared to come back up without delay. A dirty shutdown is one that lands on its back; it can not come back up without first recovering itself.

Shutdown Immediate

Perhaps the best way to initially shutdown the database is the SHUTDOWN IMMEDIATE command. This command will prevent any new logins, then rollback any uncommitted transactions, and then bring down the database. In the process of bringing down the database, Oracle will flush all the changes in memory out to the database datafiles too, just like a regular shutdown does. This makes database startup quicker. Here is an example of shutting down a database with the SHUTDOWN IMMEDIATE command:

```
SQL> shutdown immediate
```

The SHUTDOWN IMMEDIATE command will work most of the time, but there are times when it can hang and fail to shutdown the database. In these cases, the SHUTDOWN ABORT command is called for.

Shutdown Abort

The SHUTDOWN ABORT command is pretty much a guaranteed way to get the database to shutdown. It is a hard crash of the database, and this can result in a longer time to restart the database. Still, the database really cannot be hurt using the SHUTDOWN ABORT command, and there will be more than a few occasions when use of the SHUTDOWN ABORT command is necessary.

A SHUTDOWN ABORT should not be the first shutdown method of choice. However, there will come times when it is called for. Here is an example using the SHUTDOWN ABORT command:

```
SQL> shutdown abort
```

It is time to switch gears and examine the Oracle data dictionary. This is where information about the database resides.

Inside the Oracle Data Dictionary

The data dictionary is full of Metadata or information about what is going on inside the database. The data dictionary is presented in the form of a number of views. The dictionary views come in two primary forms:

VIEW	DESCRIPTION
The DBA, ALL or USER views	These views are used to manage database structures.
The v$ Dynamic Performance Views	These views are used to monitor real time database statistics

Table 3.1: *Dictionary Views*

Throughout the rest of this book the data dictionary views that will be used to manage the database will be introduced. An entire list of Oracle Data Dictionary views can be found in the Oracle documentation at <u>tahiti.oracle.com</u>.

There are hundreds of views in the data dictionary. To see the depth of the data dictionary views, here are the views that store data about Oracle tables:

- *dba_all_tables*
- *dba_indexes*
- *dba_ind_partitions*
- *dba_ind_subpartitions*
- *dba_object_tables*
- *dba_part_col_statistics*
- *dba_subpart_col_statistics*
- *dba_tables*
- *dba_tab_cols*

- *dba_tab_columns*

- *dba_tab_col_statistics*

- *dba_tab_partitions*

- *dba_tab_subpartitions*

Later in this chapter, simple data dictionary scripts will be introduced to see information about the internal structure of the datafiles, tablespaces, tables, and indexes.

⌨ To learn more about the data dictionary, get the free Oracle 10g data dictionary reference by Rampant using the Google search phrase: **bc free 10g poster**.

⌨ For a collection of pre-written Oracle data dictionary scripts, see www.oracle-script.com or use the Google search phrase: **bc oracle dictionary scripts**.

> 🔔 **Tip:** The DICT or DICTIONARY view can also be queried to see a list of all views and comments about them that exist in the data dictionary. This view is a quick way to find specific information in the data dictionary.

The Oracle initialization parameter file

When the Oracle database is started, one of the first things it needs to do is read the database initialization parameter file. The *init.ora* parameter file is created by the DBA and defines the overall instance configuration, such as how much memory should be allocated to the instance, the file locations, and internal optimization parameters.

Here is a sample *init.ora* file:

```
db_cache_size = 176000M
db_2k_cache_size = 2048M
```

```
db_16k_cache_size = 99000M
db_keep_cache_size = 600000M
db_recycle_cache_size = 64000M
shared_pool_size = 14000M
```

In this section, this database parameter file will be examined in more detail. First, the two different types of parameter files that can be used will be explored, PFILE's and SPFILE's, followed by a look at the parameters that are maintained in the database parameter file. Finally, the topic of how to manage the initialization parameter file will be covered.

Introducing the PFILE and SPFILE

Oracle provides two different types of mutually exclusive parameter files that can be used, PFILE and SPFILE. The following sections will examine these files in a bit more detail.

Parameters

The initialization parameters are a very important part of the Oracle database. Oracle reads the initialization parameter values from either a PFILE or SPFILE as the database is starting. The parameters tell the Oracle programs how much memory to allocate, where to put files related to the database and the location of existing datafiles.

A parameter has a name and a value. In this example, there is a parameter named *db_block_size*. This parameter tells oracle how big each individual block in the database is. In this case, each block is 8192 bytes, or 8k, in size.

```
db_block_size=8192
```

The next parameter is the *background_dump_dest* parameter. This parameter defines the location of Oracle trace files or log files that are created by the Oracle background processes and the important *alert log* where database messages reside. In this case, all files written by Oracle background processes will be in the /u01/oracle/admin/mydb/bdump directory.

```
background_dump_dest=/u01/oracle/admin/mydb/bdump
```

Information on all the Oracle database parameters can be found at Oracle's web site, tahiti.oracle.com. They will all be listed in the reference guide, with the exception of the undocumented hidden parameters. These parameters, while changeable, should only be modified with the aid of an experienced DBA or Oracle Technical Support also knows as MetaLink.

Some parameters are dynamic and they can be changed while the database is running. For example, the database buffer cache can be decreased in many cases while the database instance is running with the ALTER SYSTEM command:

```
alter system set db_recovery_file_dest_size=10g;
```

In this example, the parameter *db_recovery_file_dest* was dynamically changed to a value of 10 gigabytes (10g). The database will maintain this parameter until it is rebooted, unless a SPFILE is used. SPFILE's will be covered shortly.

The PFILE

Parameters are stored in either a PFILE or an SPFILE. The PFILE is a text-based file generally called the *init.ora* file which has been around for over a decade. Inside the PFILE are a number of database settings called parameters. These parameters help the Oracle programs know how to start. The parameters tell the Oracle programs how much memory to allocate, where to put files related to the database, and where certain database files already exist.

As the PFILE is text based, one can edit it in an editor like *vi* on UNIX or Notepad on Windows. When it is changed, make sure to save the changes to disk before exiting the editor. Also, make sure to save it as a plain text file, since some editors such as Microsoft Word can save documents in special formats that Oracle would not be able to read.

Depending on which operating system being used, the PFILE is located by default in the ORACLE HOME\database, which is usually the case on Windows, or ORACLE HOME\dbs directory for most other platforms.

If a PFILE is being used, it takes on the form of *initSID.ora*, meaning the file will use the *oracle_sid* that was defined when the database was created. If the SID is called *testdb*, the resulting PFILE should be called *inittestdb.ora*.

The SPFILE

The SPFILE is different from the PFILE in that it can not be directly edited. This is because it has a header and footer that contain binary values. Since an SPFILE file cannot be changed directly, Oracle allows it to be managed via the *alter system* command.

That might sound a bit more complex, but it really is no harder than manually changing a PFILE. For using an SPFILE, one can reap great benefits. It can be backed up by RMAN, Oracle's backup and recovery software, every time a change is made or when the database is backed up, which means it is easier to recover. RMAN will be covered a great deal in a later chapter! Also, SPFILES allow dynamic changes to be made to parameters that are persistent. For example, this database parameter change is not persistent if PFILES are being used:

```
Alter system set db_recovery_file_dest_size=10g;
```

If SPFILES are being used, the parameter would keep the same value, even after a database restart. This means that the parameter value only needs to be changed in one place and that it will not have to also be changed in the PFILE of the database.

One of the most important benefits of the SPFILE is that Oracle has introduced many automatic tuning features into the core of the database. Without an SPFILE, Oracle cannot autotune the database.

An SPFILE uses the same formatting for its file name as the PFILE, except the word *spfile* replaces *init*. For instance, if the *oracle_sid* is *testdb*, the resulting *spfile* would be called *spfiletestdb.ora*.

Administering the PFILE and SPFILE

As a DBA the main thing to be concerned with regarding the SPFILE and PFILES is backing them up. RMAN can be used to backup an SPFILE, or they can be backed up manually.

Remember that a PFILE is simply a text based file, which means it can be copied to another directory without affecting the Oracle instance. This is the easiest way to backup a PFILE.

To back up an SPFILE, it first needs to be converted to a PFILE. This command can accomplish that:

```
SQL> create pfile from spfile;
```

This will create a PFILE named *initSID.ora* in the $ORACLE_HOME/database directory in Windows or $ORACLE_HOME/dbs directory in Linux/Unix.

Note that the SID in *initSID.ora* will be replaced with the SID of the database as defined during creation.

In addition, the file can be backed up directly to the preferred location with the command:

```
SQL> create pfile=/path/to/backup.ora from spfile;
```

If the time comes that the SPFILE needs to be put back into place, this command can be used:

```
SQL>  create spfile from pfile=/path/to/backup.ora
```

If the database is currently running using the SPFILE, be sure to shut down first so Oracle can replace the file. As the SPFILE is in use the entire time the database is running, it should never be overwritten during normal operations.

The *v$parameter* dynamic view can be used to see the current setting of the different database parameters. In this example, the DESC SQL*Plus command is used to describe the *v$parameter* view. Then the *v$parameter* view is queried to see the value of the *control_file* parameter setting:

```
SQL> desc v$parameter

 Name                                    Null?    Type
 --------------------------------------- -------- -------------
 NUM                                              NUMBER
 NAME                                             VARCHAR2(80)
 TYPE                                             NUMBER
 VALUE                                            VARCHAR2(512)
 DISPLAY_VALUE                                    VARCHAR2(512)
 ISDEFAULT                                        VARCHAR2(9)
 ISSES_MODIFIABLE                                 VARCHAR2(5)
 ISSYS_MODIFIABLE                                 VARCHAR2(9)
 ISINSTANCE_MODIFIABLE                            VARCHAR2(5)
 ISMODIFIED                                       VARCHAR2(10)
 ISADJUSTED                                       VARCHAR2(5)
 ISDEPRECATED                                     VARCHAR2(5)
 DESCRIPTION                                      VARCHAR2(255)
 UPDATE_COMMENT                                   VARCHAR2(255)
 HASH                                             NUMBER
```

```
SQL> select name, value from v$parameter where name =
'control_files';

NAME                    VALUE
--------------------    ---------------------------------------------
control_files
C:\ORACLE\ORADATA\BOOKTST\BOOKTST\CONTROL01.CTL, C:\ORACLE
                        \ORADATA\BOOKTST\BOOKTST\CONTROL02.CTL,
C:\ORACLE\ORADATA\
                        BOOKTST\BOOKTST\CONTROL03.CTL
```

The shortcut show parameter command can also be used. For instance:

```
SQL> show parameter control_files;
```

The Parameter File at Startup Time

Oracle prefers the use of an SPFILE to a PFILE. When the Oracle database is started up, Oracle will scan the contents of the parameter directory, $ORACLE_HOME/database on Windows or the Linux directory name $ORACLE_HOME/dbs, searching in the following order:

- *spfileSID.ora*

- *spfile.ora*

- *initSID.ora*

- *init.ora*

If the directory contains none of the above, then the startup will fail. Alternatively, Oracle can be told where to find a PFILE if it is stored in a different location.

```
SQL> startup pfile=/path/to/pfile/inittestdb.ora
```

Furthermore, a PFILE can be created that contains nothing but the following line:

```
SPFILE=/path/to/spfiletestdb.ora
```

By doing so, startup can be accomplished using a PFILE in any location, but continue to use an SPFILE that can also be in a different location. This can be very beneficial for those that wish to store their SPFILE in a centralized location, such as a SAN. Now, it is time to take a quick look at redo log administration.

Administering Oracle Redo Logs

The Oracle redo log files were introduced in an earlier chapter. They are files that are like Oracle's little tape recorder, and Oracle records almost everything that happens inside the Oracle database. Oracle uses these redo log groups to recover the database, so they are pretty important.

Each individual redo log is assigned to a group. Oracle writes to only one online redo log group at a time. Once the online redo log(s) in that group are filled then Oracle will switch to writing the next online redo log group, and so on in a circular fashion.

Each online redo log is assigned a unique sequence number. No online redo log will ever have the same sequence number in a given database unless a new incarnation of that database is created. A new incarnation of a database can occur as the result of certain incomplete recovery operations; however, the DBA will not normally need to worry about conflicts in thread numbers unless an incomplete recovery of the database has been performed. Recovery will be covered in more detail later in this book.

Each online redo log group can be multiplexed. This means that each redo log group can consist of more than one online redo log file. Each file is known as a member. Each member should be located on a different disk, to protect the group from loosing all of its members in the event of a disk failure. Oracle writes to those members in parallel, to ensure that the database is always recoverable while maintaining performance.

The online redo logs are first created when the database is created, and the database cannot function without them. If all members of the active redo log group are lost, the database crashes, and worse yet, there *will* be data loss. Hence, it is very important to preserve these files. There are two kinds of redo logs that will be considered in this section, the online redo logs and archived redo logs.

First, the administration of online redo logs will be addressed. This includes creation and removal of an online redo log group, as well as the addition and removal of redo log group members.

Create Online Redo Log Groups

The ALTER DATABASE command can be used to add an online redo log group, and its associated members, to the database. Here is an example of the creation of a new online redo log group:

```
alter database add logfile group 4
'c:\oracle\oradata\booktst\booktst\redo04.log' size 50m;
```

Multiple members can be added at the same time:

```
alter database add logfile group 5
('c:\oracle\oradata\booktst\booktst\redo05a.log',
 'd:\oracle\oradata\booktst\booktst\redo05b.log') size 50m;
```

Drop an Online Redo Log Group

Of course, there are times when a given redo log group will need to be dropped. This is commonly done if there is a need to increase or reduce the size of the online redo logs. The online redo log group is dropped using the ALTER DATABASE DROP LOGFILE GROUP command as seen in this example:

```
alter database drop logfile group 5;
```

There are a few things to note concerning the dropping of redo log groups. For starters, the current redo log group cannot be dropped; meaning, if the log group that needs to be dropped is currently being written to, dropping it will not be allowed. In this case, it will be necessary to switch to the next redo log group and then drop the old one. This can be done with the following command:

```
SQL> alter system switch logfile;
```

Another thing to note is that when the redo log group is dropped from the database, it is not dropped on the file system. It must be removed manually from the file system AFTER it has been removed gracefully from the database.

Add a Member to an Online Redo Log

Sometimes an additional member needs to be added to an online redo log. Usually this occurs when there is only one member in each of the online redo groups. If a DBA finds that this is the case and is not horrified, then he does not yet understand why online redo logs are multiplexed.

The alter database command is used to add a member to a redo log group as seen in this example:

```
alter database
add logfile member 'c:\oracle\oradata\booktst\booktst\redo03a.log'
to group 3;
```

Drop a Member from an Online Redo Log

Mistakes happen, and sometimes a member needs to be removed from an online redo log group. The alter database command can be used to perform this operation too:

```
alter database
drio logfile member 'c:\oracle\oradata\booktst\booktst\redo03a.log'
;
```

Again, when a member of a redo log group is dropped, the file will not be dropped from the OS itself. This must be done manually at the operating system level.

Online Redo Log Data Dictionary Views

Oracle provides data dictionary views for the online redo logs as seen in this table:

VIEW NAME	DESCRIPTION
v$log	Lists information about each member of each online redo log group.
v$logfile	Provides redo log file name information

Table 3.2: *Online redo log data dictionary views*

If *v$log* is queried, information about each redo log group can be seen, including the size of each member and how many members are in each log group. Most importantly, it is possible to determine which log group is the current redo log group. Remember the ALTER SYSTEM SWITCH LOGFILE command can be used to switch from one log group to another.

Here is a dictionary query to display the logs:

```
set lines 120;
set pages 999;

select substr(time,1,5) day,
```

```
to_char(sum(decode(substr(time,10,2),'00',1,0)),'99') "00",
to_char(sum(decode(substr(time,10,2),'01',1,0)),'99') "01",
to_char(sum(decode(substr(time,10,2),'02',1,0)),'99') "02",
to_char(sum(decode(substr(time,10,2),'03',1,0)),'99') "03",
to_char(sum(decode(substr(time,10,2),'04',1,0)),'99') "04",
to_char(sum(decode(substr(time,10,2),'05',1,0)),'99') "05",
to_char(sum(decode(substr(time,10,2),'06',1,0)),'99') "06",
to_char(sum(decode(substr(time,10,2),'07',1,0)),'99') "07",
to_char(sum(decode(substr(time,10,2),'08',1,0)),'99') "08",
to_char(sum(decode(substr(time,10,2),'09',1,0)),'99') "09",
to_char(sum(decode(substr(time,10,2),'10',1,0)),'99') "10",
to_char(sum(decode(substr(time,10,2),'11',1,0)),'99') "11",
to_char(sum(decode(substr(time,10,2),'12',1,0)),'99') "12",
to_char(sum(decode(substr(time,10,2),'13',1,0)),'99') "13",
to_char(sum(decode(substr(time,10,2),'14',1,0)),'99') "14",
to_char(sum(decode(substr(time,10,2),'15',1,0)),'99') "15",
to_char(sum(decode(substr(time,10,2),'16',1,0)),'99') "16",
to_char(sum(decode(substr(time,10,2),'17',1,0)),'99') "17",
to_char(sum(decode(substr(time,10,2),'18',1,0)),'99') "18",
to_char(sum(decode(substr(time,10,2),'19',1,0)),'99') "19",
to_char(sum(decode(substr(time,10,2),'20',1,0)),'99') "20",
to_char(sum(decode(substr(time,10,2),'21',1,0)),'99') "21",
to_char(sum(decode(substr(time,10,2),'22',1,0)),'99') "22",
to_char(sum(decode(substr(time,10,2),'23',1,0)),'99') "23"
from v$log_history
group by substr(time,1,5);
```

Administer the Archived Redo Logs

An Oracle database can run in one of two modes. By default, the database is created in NOARCHIVELOG mode. When in NOARCHIVELOG mode the database runs normally, but there is no capacity to perform any type of point in time recovery operations or online backups. Thus, the database has to be shutdown to back it up, and when it needs to be recovered the database can only be recovered to the point of the last backup. While this might be fine for a development environment, the big corporate types tend to frown when a weeks worth of current production accounting data is lost forever.

Using the ARCHIVELOG Mode

So, to avoid the wrath of the CEO and angry end-users, the savvy DBA will want to run Oracle in ARCHIVELOG mode. In ARCHIVELOG mode, the database will make copies of all online redo logs after they are filled. These copies are called archived redo logs. The archived redo logs are created via the ARCH process. The ARCH process copies the archived redo log files to one or more archive log destination directories.

The use of ARCHIVELOG mode requires some configuration of the database. The database must be put in ARCHIVELOG mode, the ARCH process must be configured, and the archived redo log destination directories must be prepared.

There are some down sides to running the database in ARCHIVELOG mode. For example, once an online redo log has been filled, it cannot be reused until it has been archived. If Oracle cannot archive the online redo log because the destination directory for the archived redo logs is full, it will switch to the next online redo log and keep working. At the same time, Oracle will continue to try to archive the log file.

Unfortunately, once the database runs out of available online redo logs, there is a problem. If the log files cannot be written out, Oracle would have to overwrite them. This is not good because it means the data that was in those files would be lost since Oracle could not archive the file. As a result, in an effort to protect the database, Oracle will not overwrite data in an online redo log file until that log file has been archived. Until the file has been archived, the database will simply stop processing user requests. Once the log file has been archived, the database will be freed, and processing can proceed as normal.

At this point, it should be apparent how an incorrect configuration of the database, when it is in ARCHIVELOG mode, can eventually lead to the database suspending operations because it can not archive the current online redo logs.

The next sections will look at how to configure the database for ARCHIVELOG mode and how to put the database in ARCHIVELOG mode.

Configuring the database for ARCHIVELOG Mode

One of the main features of a database that is in ARCHIVELOG mode is that it generates copies of the online redo logs called archived redo logs. By default, in version 10g, Oracle will send archived redo logs to the flash recovery area and experts also recommended this configuration.

⌗ Type the following string into the Google search engine to find more information: **bc oracle archivelog**.

To properly setup the flash recovery area, the two parameters shown in the following table should be set as indicated:

PARAMETER	DEFAULT VALUE	MEANING
db_recovery_file_dest	$ORACLE_BASE/ flash_recovery_area	This is the location of the flash recovery area.
db_recovery_file_dest_size	2g	This is the maximum size that can be used by the flash recovery area. If this size limit is exceeded, space must be cleared or database operations will eventually stall.

Table 3.3: *Flash recovery area parameters*

The default values for these parameters can be changed using the ALTER SYSTEM command. Examples of the use of the ALTER SYSTEM command to change parameters can be found earlier in this chapter. Savvy DBA's recommend that the *db_recovery_file_dest* parameter be set to a directory location that is separate from the location of the Oracle software, the redo logs, and the data files. It is not a good idea to accidentally fill up

ORACLE_HOME or cause performance issues due to contention.

When the flash recovery area is configured, a directory for the database will be created in the location defined by the *db_recovery_file_dest* parameter. The example database has a directory called:

```
C:\Oracle\product\flash_recovery_area\BOOKTST
```

Under this directory are individual directories for various file types such as ARCHIVELOG where the archived redo logs will reside.

In earlier versions of Oracle a special Oracle process called ARCH had to be enabled by setting another parameter. Oracle Database 10g does not require this. When the database is in ARCHIVELOG mode, it will start the ARCH process automatically.

Putting the database in ARCHIVELOG Mode

Once the flash recovery area has been configured, the database can be put in ARCHIVELOG mode. Unfortunately, this requires that the database be shutdown first with the SHUTDOWN command. Refer to the section earlier in the chapter that recommended using SHUTDOWN IMMEDIATE. Once the database has been shutdown, the database should be started in mount mode with the STARTUP MOUNT command. Then put the database in ARCHIVELOG mode, and finally open the database. Here is an example of how this all works from the command line:

```
SQL> shutdown immediate
Database closed.
Database dismounted.
ORACLE instance shut down.
```

```
SQL> startup mount
ORACLE instance started.

Total System Global Area  272629760 bytes
Fixed Size                   788472 bytes
Variable Size             103806984 bytes
Database Buffers          167772160 bytes
Redo Buffers                 262144 bytes
Database mounted.
SQL> alter database archivelog;

Database altered.

SQL> alter database open;

Database altered.
```

Once the database is in ARCHIVELOG mode, it will start generating archived redo logs. It is always a good idea to make sure that the archived redo logs are getting generated. To do this, first force a log switch with the ALTER SYSTEM SWITCH LOGFILE command. Then check the flash recovery area to make sure an archived redo log is created.

The archived redo logs will be in the flash recovery area in the ARCHIVELOG directory. Under that directory there will be individual directories, each represents a different date such as 2005_03_09 for March 3, 2005. The directory structure on an example computer may look like this:

```
C:\Oracle\product\flash_recovery_area\BOOKTST\ARCHIVELOG\2005_03_09
```

It might look a little different on different computers. Sometimes Oracle does different things on different Operating Systems; however, it should be pretty easy to figure it out.

Now, navigate to the directory that is named for today's date. Next, perform a directory listing in that directory and the archived redo logs should be visible in the directory. Here is an example of what might appear:

```
C:\Oracle\product\flash_recovery_area\BOOKTST\ARCHIVELOG\2005_03_16>
dir
 Volume in drive C has no label.
 Volume Serial Number is 50FD-2353

 Directory of
 c:\Oracle\product\flash_recovery_area\BOOKTST\ARCHIVELOG\2005_03_16

03/16/2005  10:54 PM    <DIR>          .
03/16/2005  10:54 PM    <DIR>          ..
03/16/2005  12:00 AM        51,222,016 O1_MF_1_195_13HLW5YL_.ARC
03/16/2005  12:01 AM        10,018,304 O1_MF_1_196_13HLXR1L_.ARC
03/16/2005  12:15 AM        10,018,304 O1_MF_1_197_13HMQRYV_.ARC
03/16/2005  12:20 AM        10,018,304 O1_MF_1_198_13HN0QFF_.ARC
03/16/2005  05:32 AM        51,229,184 O1_MF_1_199_13J6BN6V_.ARC
03/16/2005  06:27 AM        10,018,304 O1_MF_1_200_13J9L165_.ARC
03/16/2005  07:05 AM        10,017,792 O1_MF_1_201_13JCS3M9_.ARC
03/16/2005  08:00 AM        10,018,304 O1_MF_1_202_13JH070P_.ARC
03/16/2005  01:21 PM        51,229,184 O1_MF_1_203_13K1SMTD_.ARC
03/16/2005  02:21 PM        10,018,304 O1_MF_1_204_13K5B67B_.ARC
03/16/2005  03:28 PM        10,018,304 O1_MF_1_205_13K973FT_.ARC
03/16/2005  04:31 PM        10,018,304 O1_MF_1_206_13KDY5G2_.ARC
03/16/2005  09:49 PM        51,229,184 O1_MF_1_207_13KZLJ4D_.ARC
03/16/2005  10:54 PM        10,018,304 O1_MF_1_208_13L3DMJK_.ARC
              14 File(s)     305,092,096 bytes
               2 Dir(s)  49,594,761,216 bytes free
```

If files are being generated here, archiving is working right.

Type the following string into the Google search engine to find more information: **bc oracle rman.**

Archived Redo Log Data Dictionary Views

Oracle provides data dictionary views for the archived redo logs as seen in this table:

VIEW NAME	DESCRIPTION
v$archived_log	Information about archived redo logs.
v$parameter	Shows the location of the flash recovery area where archived redo logs are created.
v$log_history	Contains information on previous redo logs

Table 3.4: *Data dictionary views for archived redo logs*

Administering Oracle UNDO

Oracle allows changes to be made to the database in kind of a "try it before you buy it mode." What this means is that the changes that are made by a particular user can only be seen that user at first. Hence, a user can make changes and check those changes to make sure they are ok before anyone else is able to see them. Once the user is sure their changes are correct, the COMMIT command is issued, and everyone else can then see them.

This type of functionality yields database consistency. This means that the data in the database, when it is queried, is always consistent to the same point in time. For example, if two tables are queried at the same time, tables named PARENT and CHILD for instance, the query will produce records from both tables as they looked at the same point in time. This means that no one can slip a record into the CHILD table while the PARENT table is being read, or vice versa. The assurance that the records that will be read will be consistent to the same point in time is known as read consistency. Read consistency produces a query's results as they were the moment Enter was pressed.

Oracle Undo segments support these read consistent operations as well as other database operations such as flashback operations which will be covered later in this book. Oracle creates an undo segment in the SYSTEM tablespace when the database is created. This undo segment only supports operations in the SYSTEM tablespace. Hence, if other tablespaces are going to be used, which is highly recommended, other undo segments will be needed.

So, where do these other undo segments come from? An undo tablespace is created with the CREATE UNDO TABLESPACE command and Oracle Database 10g will create and manage the

---

undo segments automatically. Tablespaces will be covered in more detail next.

When an Oracle Database is first created, an undo tablespace can be created at that time, and this is the recommended approach. Before the undo tablespace can be used, a few parameters need to be set. There are those parameters again, they show up everywhere! Here is a list of parameters the need to be considered:

PARAMETER	DEFAULT VALUE	MEANING
undo_management	auto – The recommended setting is auto. Using automated undo segments rather than manual segments is also recommended.	Tells Oracle if it should use manual or automatic undo management.
undo_retention	900	Determines how long Oracle will try to preserve the generated undo.
undo_tablespace	The first available undo tablespace in the database	This is the name of the undo tablespace to be used. Only one undo tablespace can be used at any time.

Table 3.5: *Undo tablespace parameters*

The ALTER SYSTEM command can be used to change any of the parameters listed above at any time. However, please note that if the undo tablespace is changed by altering the *undo_tablespace* parameter, there still may be active transactions against the old tablespace. Keep that in mind before dropping it since it could result in one of the DBA's most common errors: ORA-01555, snapshot too old, rollback segment too small!

Administering Tablespaces

Since tablespaces have been introduced, it is time to fill in some of the details. A tablespace is where the physical Oracle meets the logical Oracle. A tablespace is a bit like a file system for the database. It is a logical entity that provides storage space so that users can create things like tables and indexes. This means that the tablespace only exists within the Oracle database itself. Its characteristics include a name, and one or more datafiles that are assigned to it at creation time. Hence, the total space available in a tablespace is the total size of the pre-allocated datafiles assigned to the tablespace. One datafile can only be assigned to one tablespace, so there is no co-habitation of datafiles amongst tablespaces.

There are two types of tablespaces, dictionary managed and locally managed. Locally managed tablespaces should always be used in Oracle Database 10g, and this is the default tablespace type. Only locally managed tablespaces will be covered in this book.

🖳 Type the following string into the Google search engine to find more information: **bc oracle lmt.**

Creating and dropping tablespaces will be covered in this section first. Then how to alter tablespaces will be examined and finally the topic of which data dictionary views can be used to manage tablespaces and their associated datafiles will be covered.

Creating Tablespaces

Tablespaces are created with the CREATE TABLESPACE command. Before creating the tablespace one should decide:

- How big the tablespace is to be.

- Where to put the datafile or datafiles that will be associated with that tablespace.

- What to call the tablespace and the datafiles.

Experts recommend that the following be included in the datafile name:

- The name of the database

- The name of the tablespace

- A number that makes the datafile unique

So, for a tablespace called USERS assigned to a database called BOOKTST, there would be a datafile called *booktst_users_01.dbf*. Here is an example of creating such a tablespace using the CREATE TABLESPACE command:

```
Create tablespace users
Datafile '/ora01/oracle/oradata/booktst_users_01.dbf' size 50m;
```

Note that 50m was used to indicate that the tablespace should be 50 megabytes in size. The k symbol can be used for kilobytes and the g symbol for gigabytes.

By default, Oracle tablespaces will not grow if they run out of space. If all the space is used, the DBA is just out of luck unless the *autoextend* keyword was used to indicate that the tablespace may grow dynamically. Here is an example of creating a tablespace that is set to *autoextend*:

```
create tablespace
    users
datafile
    '/ora01/oracle/oradata/booktst_users_01.dbf' size 50m
autoextend on
next 10m
maxsize 100m;
```

In this example, the tablespace will auto extend in increments of 10 megabytes until it reaches a maximum size of 100 megabytes.

Exerts recommend that auto extend be used on all tablespaces for any production database.

Dropping Tablespaces

Sometimes it may be necessary to get rid of tablespaces. The drop tablespace command is used for such an operation. In this example, the USELESS tablespace is going to be dropped from the database:

```
Drop tablespace useless;
```

Oracle is pretty smart, and it will generate an error if there is anything in a tablespace when an attempt is made to drop it. If this is the case, Oracle can be told to remove all objects in the tablespace with the INCLUDING CONTENTS keyword as seen here:

```
Drop tablespace useless including contents;
```

By default, Oracle does not clean up after itself, but there is an option to force it to clean up after itself with the INCLUDING CONTENTS and DATAFILES keywords as seen in this example:

```
Drop tablespace useless including contents and datafiles;
```

Using this command will drop the tablespace, any and all objects within it, and all associated data files on the hard disk.

BE CAREFUL. If a tablespace is dropped, it is very difficult to bring the tables back. A high quality backup plan must be in place to get the data back, and even then data will be lost unless extraordinary measures are taken during recovery.

Altering Tablespaces

The ALTER TABLESPACE command allows the modification of tablespace characteristics. The ALTER TABLESPACE command can be used to add datafiles, indicate the beginning and ending of online backups, and other operations as required. Here is an example of the use of the ALTER TABLESPACE command to rename the BADNAME tablespace name to GOODNAME:

```
ALTER TABLESPACE badname RENAME TO goodname;
```

Use the following command to add a datafile to a tablespace:

```
ALTER TABLESPACE users ADD DATAFILE
'/ora01/oracle/oradata/booktst_users_02.dbf' size 100m
```

Use the following command to resize a datafile:

```
ALTER DATABASE DATAFILE /ora01/oracle/oradata/booktst_users_02.dbf'
resize 150M
```

Temporary Tablespaces

Temporary tablespaces are used for special operations, particularly for sorting data results on disk. For SQL with millions of rows returned, the sort operation is too large for the RAM area and must occur on disk. The temporary tablespace is where this takes place.

Each database should have one temporary tablespace that is created when the database is created. Temporary tablespaces are created, dropped and managed with the CREATE TEMPORARY TABLESPACE, DROP TEMPORARY TABLESPACE, and ALTER TEMPORARY TABLESPACE commands, each of which is like it's CREATE TABLESPACE counterpart.

The only other difference is that a temporary tablespace uses temporary files, also called tempfiles, rather than regular datafiles. Thus, instead of using the datafiles keyword the tempfiles keyword is used when issuing a CREATE, DROP or ALTER TABLESPACE command as can be seen in these examples:

```
CREATE TEMPORARY TABLESPACE temp
TEMPFILE '/ora01/oracle/oradata/booktst_temp_01.dbf' SIZE 50m;

DROP TEMPORARY TABLESPACE temp INCLUDING CONTENTS AND DATAFILES;
```

Tempfiles are a bit different than datafiles in that they may not immediately grow to the size that they have been allocated. This particular functionality is platform dependent. Hence, there is no need to panic if the file looks too small.

Tablespace Data Dictionary Views

Oracle provides data dictionary views for tablespaces in the database. They are:

VIEW NAME	DESCRIPTION
dba_tablespaces	Describes each tablespace
dba_data_files	Lists each datafile in the database.
dba_temp_files	Describes each tempfile in the database.

Table 3.6: *Tablespace data dictionary views*

Conclusion

It is finally time to create objects to store in the database. These objects can include tables, indexes, and many other types of segments. This chapter has defined the base foundation that a database must have. Adding tables, inserting rows, and so on cannot occur without the different structures that have been defined here.

Just think of it this way: the house is built and it is finally ready to be customized! The foundation is in place, the boards are up, and the drywall is finally in place. Now it is time to put a few things in it and really put it to use.

The main points of this chapter include:

- Oracle allows for the creation of logical tablespaces which are a logical collection of one-or-more physical disk datafiles.

- Oracle has temporary tablespace that are used to sort large results from SQL statements.

The next chapter will dive in to see how to administer the tables and indexes within the Oracle database.

Administering Oracle Objects and Constraints

One of the main responsibilities of Oracle DBA's is the creation of objects and constraints within the database. Once the databases and tablespaces have been created, then objects can be created. Objects are things stored inside the database. They are used to store data and to make accessing that data faster and easier. This chapter first introduces the management of basic Oracle objects such as tables and indexes. It will then introduce the management of Oracle constraints.

Administering Oracle Objects and Constraints

One thing to mention is that before creating objects, a user account should first be created that will be used to create these objects. The newly created Oracle database does come with a few users already built in, for example, SYS and SYSTEM. These accounts are system management accounts or sample accounts, and really are not designed to be used to create objects. The DBA should create a special user in which to create objects. How to create users will be covered in the next chapter.

For the examples in this chapter, the SCOTT user will be used.

Administering Oracle Tables

Oracle Tables are the bookshelves of Oracle. This is where Oracle stores the data. This section will cover what tables are for, and then how to create, alter and drop Oracle tables.

Oracle Tables

Tables are used to store data. Tables as assigned a name when they are created. This name should describe what data is stored in the table, such as cars, employees or addresses. A table is created using the CREATE TABLE command. When created, the table is assigned to a tablespace.

Think of a table like a spreadsheet in a way. It has columns, which are defined when the table is created. Each column is given a name to describe the data that is contained in the column. Each column is also assigned a datatype, which indicates what kind of data may be stored in the column.

For example, to store letters in the table, the datatype a *varchar2* would be used. varchar stands for varying character, which means the column data can vary in length. A *varchar2* also can hold numeric characters.

To store numbers, the column will be a *number* type. To store date/time stamps, the column type would be *date*.

⚏ Type the following string into the Google search engine to find more information: **bc oracle create table.**

The following table lists the basic data types that will be used when dealing with tables as a beginning DBA:

DATATYPE	EXAMPLE	DESCTIPTION
CHAR	CHAR(5)	This is a fixed length character column. In the example, it will always be 5 characters in length, even if it's empty.
DATE	DATE	This is a date column. It stores both the date (with century) and time in it.

DATATYPE	EXAMPLE	DESCTIPTION
NUMBER	NUMBER (5) NUMBER(5,2) NUMBER	This is a number column. Note that the number of decimal points a given number has can be defined as well as how big the number can be. In the first example, the number can only have 5 digits in it (99999). In the second, it can have 5 digits, but 2 of those are after the decimal point (999.99). Finally, the last number is unbounded.
VARCHAR2	VARCHAR2(30)	This is a character column that can vary in length. This is good, because it means that the column is probably going to take up less space overall than one defined as a char(30). For example, if the character string "This is a test" is put into a char(30) column, it would always take up 30 bytes. If it is put into a varchar2(30) column, it would only take up 14 bytes. This difference can be big when there is a lot of data to be stored.

Table 4.1: *Datatypes*

There are other data types, but these are good ones with which to start.

Creating Tables

Before tables can be used, they have to be created and this is generally the job of the DBA. Creating tables is done with the CREATE TABLE command. The CREATE TABLE command does the following:

- Defines the table name

- Defines the columns in the table and the datatypes of those columns

- Defines what tablespace the table resides in (optional)

- Defines other characteristics of the table (optional)

Here is an example of the CREATE TABLE command in action:

```
Connect scott/tiger

CREATE TABLE books
( book_id            NUMBER PRIMARY KEY,
  book_name          VARCHAR2(30),
  author_name        VARCHAR2(40),
  book_isbn          VARCHAR2(20) )
TABLESPACE users;
```

In this example, a table called BOOKS is created which has 4 columns. The first column is BOOK_ID and is a NUMBER datatype. This means numbers will be stored in this column.

Notice that the keyword PRIMARY KEY was included where the BOOK_ID column was defined. This is known as an in-line constraint because the constraint is being defined on the same line as the column associated with the constraint. In this case the keyword PRIMARY KEY means a primary key constraint is being defined on the BOOKS table called PK_BOOKS.

What is a primary key constraint? A constraint is a rule that is applied to the table. In this case, the primary key constraint is a rule that says a duplicate entry cannot exist in the BOOK_ID column, and the BOOK_ID column can never be empty or null. In this example, each book has a unique BOOK_ID assigned. In other words, War and Peace might have a BOOK_ID of 12345, and no other book will ever have the same BOOK_ID column value.

One might ask, why not just make the title of the book the primary key? The answer is that there might be a number of different books called *War and Peace*. One might be paperback and one might be hardcover. One might be out of print, one might be an easy to read child's version. Hence, the title of the book is not a good candidate to uniquely identify the book. In this case, there is a column called BOOK_ID that will be unique for each book. It then becomes the primary key. Since this is not a book about designing databases, that is enough on primary keys for now.

In Oracle, each primary key column must be unique. Thus, there cannot be two books with a BOOK_ID of 12345. Oracle would reject the second attempt to use that BOOK_ID and return an error to the user.

A combination of columns can also be defined to be the primary key. This is known as a concatenated primary key. These kinds of constraints are defined as out-of-line constraints because they are defined on their own line in the CREATE TABLE statement.

Here is an example of the creation of an out-of-line primary key constraint. In this case the books table might well have multiple BOOK_ID's. Hence, a sequence number will be added to the column (BOOK_ID_SEQ) to act as a tie breaker.

```
CREATE TABLE books
( book_id              NUMBER,
  book_id_seq          NUMBER,
  book_name            VARCHAR2(30),
  author_name          VARCHAR2(40),
  book_isbn            VARCHAR2(20),
  CONSTRAINT
    pk_books
  PRIMARY KEY (book_id, book_id_seq) )
TABLESPACE users;
```

Once the table is created, the SQL*Plus DESC command can be used to see its structure as shown in this example:

```
SQL>desc books

Name                                      Null?     Type
----------------------------------------- -------- ------------
 BOOK_ID                                   NOT NULL NUMBER
 BOOK_ID_SEQ                               NOT NULL NUMBER
 BOOK_NAME                                          VARCHAR2(30)
 AUTHOR_NAME                                        VARCHAR2(40)
 BOOK_ISBN                                          VARCHAR2(20)
```

Note that the BOOK_ID and BOOK_ID_SEQ columns have a NOT NULL constraint assigned to them. Any time a column is assigned to a table's primary key, it will be given a NOT NULL constraint. As a result, no primary key column can be NULL.

Although aspiring DBA's should already know something about the SQL language, it will not hurt to have a little refresher about NULL values. A NULL is a third type of logic. In two value logic there is YES and NO, ON and OFF, or TRUE and FALSE. Relational databases deal in three value logic, and the third value is always NULL. Hence, now there is YES, NO and NULL or TRUE, FALSE and NULL.

NULL values impact the way SQL statements are written. If the column can be NULL, and if that column is going to be used in a WHERE clause, then those clauses have to be carefully written. This is because a statement like WHERE a != 1 will not evaluate to TRUE if the column is a NULL value as seen in this example:

```
SQL> CREATE TABLE test_null (id NUMBER);
Table created.
SQL> INSERT INTO test_null VALUES (1);
1 row created.
SQL> INSERT INTO test_null VALUES (2);
1 row created.
SQL> INSERT INTO test_null VALUES (NULL);
1 row created.
SQL> SELECT * FROM test_null;

        ID
----------
         1
         2

-- The select count(*) shows 3 records

SQL> SELECT COUNT(*) FROM test_null;

  COUNT(*)
----------
         3
-- select count(*) with a where clause, shows 2 records.
```

```
SQL> SELECT COUNT(*) FROM test_null WHERE id > 0;

  COUNT(*)
----------
         2
-- select count(*) with a where clause, in this case shows one
record.
SQL> SELECT COUNT(*) FROM test_null WHERE id != 1;

  COUNT(*)
----------
         1
```

When a column is defined to be NOT NULL that means it cannot have a NULL value assigned. This eliminates the problem of three valued logic very nicely, but this may not always be possible when designing tables.

There are, of course, many more advanced features revolving around tables. Issues like partitioning and index-organized tables are some advanced topics to be looked into once the basics are mastered. Also, there are other types of constraints that can be encountered such as foreign key constraints. Finally, in earlier versions of Oracle, there were physical storage characteristics related to the table. Thankfully, Oracle Database 10g takes care of a number of the physical storage requirements. There are many other advanced topics that can be researched in advanced Oracle DBA books.

With that introduction to the creation of a basic table, it is time to look at how to use the ALTER TABLE command so the characteristics of the table can be managed.

Altering Tables

Having created tables, there will be times when they will need to be altered in some respect. This is done with the ALTER TABLE command. Some functions that the ALTER TABLE command can do include:

- Moving a table to another tablespace

- Adding a column to the table

- Dropping a column from the table

- Changing a column name

- Modify existing constraints or add new constraints

For example, in order to move the BOOKS table to another tablespace, the following ALTER TABLE command allows this to be done easily:

```
ALTER TABLE books MOVE TABLESPACE new_users;
```

A column can be added to a table with the ALTER TABLE command. In this case, a column called BOOK_PRICE is being added to the BOOKS table. This column is a number data type:

```
ALTER TABLE books ADD book_price NUMBER;
```

Multiple columns can also be added as seen in the following example where columns called BOOK_PUB_NO and BOOK_ALT_TITLE are being added to the BOOKS table:

```
ALTER TABLE
   books
ADD
(
   book_pub_no    NUMBER,
   book_alt_title VARCHAR2(50)
);
```

It used to be a big deal in Oracle to rename or remove a column from a table. The data had to be saved and the table had to be dropped and recreated. This could have a tremendous impact if it was a big table in a production environment. Now, columns can be renamed or dropped from a table with the ALTER TABLE command.

The following example demonstrates renaming and dropping a column. In the first example, the BOOK_ISBN column is renamed to ISBN_NUMBER. In the second example, the BOOK_PUB_NO column is dropped:

```
ALTER TABLE books RENAME COLUMN book_isbn TO isbn_number;
ALTER TABLE books DROP COLUMN book_pub_no;
```

Primary key constraints were covered earlier in this section. Oracle actually has a number of different constraint types that will be covered in more detail later in this section. However, this would be a good time to show how to rename a constraint with the ALTER TABLE command:

```
ALTER TABLE books
RENAME CONSTRAINT pk_books TO pk_book;
```

Dropping Tables

The DROP TABLE command allows tables to be dropped from an Oracle database. In this example, the BOOKS table, which was created earlier in this chapter, is dropped:

```
DROP TABLE books;
```

Oracle 10g has a recycle bin, kind of an old table's retirement home. A table that has been dropped can be recovered from the recycle bin using the FLASHBACK TABLE command as shown here:

```
SQL> DROP TABLE books;
SQL> FLASHBACK TABLE books TO BEFORE DROP;
```

Dropped a table by accident? In Oracle Database 10g the FLASHBACK TABLE command will recover the table and many of the objects associated with the table. Some things are not recovered, such as bitmap join indexes, which are an advanced type of index that will not be covered in this book, and foreign key constraints, which will be covered in this book.

The FLASHBACK TABLE command works most of the time, though the more time that has elapsed since the table was dropped, the less likely it will be in the recycle bin. Oracle purges the recycle bin from time to time based on a number of different criteria. The contents of the recycle bin can be seen using SQL*Plus with the SHOW RECYCLEBIN command:

```
SQL> show recyclebin;

ORIGINAL NAME RECYCLEBIN NAME                     OBJECT TYPE  DROP TIME
------------- ------------------------------      -----------  ----------
BOOKS         BIN$D3XWKKUCQVq2EG8/vkjNDw==$0 TABLE            2005-05-30
```

Inside the Oracle Data Dictionary

DBA's are human and can be a bit forgetful from time to time. This is where the data dictionary is very useful. The data dictionary is a repository of Metadata about the Oracle database. Metadata is information about information, and the data dictionary is information about the database. This section will cover how to use the data dictionary to get information on tables.

Oracle provides several data dictionary views that can be used to collect information on views in the database. These views include:

- *dba_tables, all_tables, user_tables*

- *dba_tab_columns, all_tab_columns* and *user_tab_columns*

As an example, the DBA forgets where the BOOKS table is located. From the SYSTEM account, he can query the *dba_tables* view to find the table:

```
CONNECT system/your_password
SELECT owner, table_name, tablespace_name
FROM dba_tables
WHERE table_name='BOOKS';
```

The other views that help locate tables are *user_tables* and *all_tables*.

Oracle also provides views that allow the attributes of table columns to be viewed. The *dba_tab_columns* view, *all_tab_columns* view and *user_tab_columns* view yield a variety of information on table columns.

Tables and Statistics

The guys who wrote Oracle are pretty smart. One of the things they built in the database is this program called the optimizer. The optimizer's job is to take SQL statements and decide how to get the data that is being asked for in the SQL statement and how to get it in the quickest way possible.

When an SQL statement is executed, the database must convert the query into an execution plan and choose the best way to retrieve the data. For Oracle, each SQL query has many choices for execution plans, including which index to use to retrieve table row, what order in which to join multiple tables together, and which internal join methods to use. Oracle has nested loop joins, hash joins, star joins, and sort merge join methods. These execution plans are computed by the Oracle cost-based SQL optimizer commonly known as the CBO.

The choice of executions plans made by the Oracle SQL Optimizer is only as good as the Oracle statistics. To always choose the best execution plan for a SQL query, Oracle relies on information about the tables and indexes in the query.

Once the optimizer has done its job, it provides an execution plan to Oracle. An execution plan is like a set of instructions that tells Oracle how to go and get the data. Although this chapter is not about how to read execution plans, here is what a simple execution plan might look like:

Step	Operation	Object	ROWS
	SORT		100
	FULL SCAN	EMP	100

Table 4.2: *Sample execution plan*

This is a pretty simple plan. In it, the optimizer tells Oracle to first go get all the rows of the EMP department, and then sort those rows. Reading an execution plan is somewhat of an art, so have faith that the full scan of the EMP table is first.

In the plan, there is a column called ROWS. This is the number of rows that the query will process. How did Oracle know that it was going to process 100 rows? This Oracle thing is smart, isn't it?

Well, Oracle is not quite that smart. In this case, Oracle knew, or in most cases it is a good guess, that 100 rows would be processed because statistics were generated on the EMP table after the table was created. The optimizer uses these statistics to generate execution plans.

The optimizer program uses statistics on tables and on the indexes surrounding those tables, so it is important to have statistics on both. In the next section, how to generate statistics on tables and indexes in a database will be covered. Starting with the introduction of the *dbms_stats* package, Oracle provides a simple way for the Oracle professional to collect statistics for the CBO.

The old-fashioned ANALYZE TABLE and *dbms_utility* methods for generating CBO statistics are obsolete and somewhat dangerous to SQL performance because they do not always capture high-quality information about tables and indexes. The CBO uses object statistics to choose the best execution plan for all SQL statements.

The *dbms_stats* utility does a far better job in estimating statistics, especially for large partitioned tables, and better stats result in faster SQL execution plans. Here is a sample execution of *dbms_stats* with the options clause.

```
exec dbms_stats.gather_schema_stats ( -
ownname          => 'SCOTT', -
options          => 'GATHER AUTO', -
estimate_percent => dbms_stats.auto_sample_size, -
method_opt       => 'for all columns size repeat', -
degree           => 15 -
)
```

How to Generate Statistics

Oracle provides a stored procedure or program that will generate the statistics it needs. Oracle requires statistics on both tables and any associated indexes, and most of the time both can be generated with just one command.

To generate statistics, use the *dbms_stats* stored package. There are two procedures contained within the *dbms_stats* package that will be of the most interest, *dbms_stats.gather_schema_stats* and *dbms_stats.gather_table_stats*. Also, in Oracle database 10g the DBA will want to gather system statistics and fixed view statistics. Each of these operations will be covered in a bit more detail next.

There is also an ANALYZE command that can be used to generate statistics. It has been deprecated in Oracle Database 10g, which means it is not supported anymore, so it will not be covered in this book.

Using *dbms_stats.gather_schema_stats*

The *dbms_stats.gather_schema_stats* procedure allows statistics to be gathered for all objects in a give schema. This is the easiest way to generate statistics for a large number of objects. Here is an example of using the *dbms_stats.gather_schema_stats* procedure to gather statistics on the SCOTT schema of a database:

```
EXEC dbms_stats.gather_schema_stats ('SCOTT', cascade=>TRUE);
```

This command will generate statistics on all tables in the SCOTT schema. Since the CASCADE command was included, statistics will also be generated on the indexes. It is important to have statistics on indexes as well as on tables in Oracle!

Of course, this is just the basic way to run this command. Several options are available, but for now, as a new DBA, this will do. In fact, Oracle 10g automatically collects database statistics every night out of the box. At some point down the road, it will be worth investigating some of the Oracle Database 10g statistics gathering options such as histograms, and granularity.

When a new table is created, it may not be practical or desirable to re-generate statistics on the entire schema if the schema is quite large and the database is very busy. Instead, use the *dbms_stats.gather_table_stats* command to generate statistics for a single table, and optionally for related table indexes. Here is an example:

```
EXEC dbms_stats.gather_table_stats ('SCOTT','EMP',cascade=>TRUE);
```

In this case, statistics are being generated for the EMP table in the SCOTT schema. Again the *cascade* parameter was used to insure all of the indexes get analyzed.

⊞ Type the following string into the Google search engine to find more information: **bc oracle dbms_stats**

Gathering System Statistics, Data Dictionary Statistics, and Fixed Statistics

Another function of Oracle Database 10g is to generate system statistics and statistics on fixed tables. This process will be introduced in this section. Gathering system statistics will be covered first followed by how to gather statistics on fixed tables.

Gathering System Statistics

The optimizer depends on various inputs, and one of these is system derived information. This information includes disk response times and CPU response times. Oracle Database 10g uses the *dbms_stats.gather_system_stats* command to generate system statistics. System statistics are generated under normal system loads and is a three stage process:

- Start collecting statistics

- Run a representative load during the statistics collection

- Stop collecting statistics

Here is an example of this operation. The double dash (--) denotes a comment:

```
-- Run the next statement before you start running the workload
EXECUTE dbms_stats.gather_system_stats ('Start');

-- Run a typical workload here

-- Run the next statement to stop gathering statistics.
EXECUTE dbms_stats.gather_system_stats ('Stop');
```

This should only be run when things change on the system, such as when new disks are added, CPU's are added, or if the system load changes.

To fully appreciate *dbms_stats,* certain major directives need to be examined. Each of these directives will be examined in more detail next to see how they are used to gather top-quality statistics for the cost-based SQL optimizer.

The *dbms_stats options* parameter

Using one of the four provided methods, this option governs the way Oracle statistics are refreshed:

- *gather* – Reanalyzes the whole schema

- *gather empty* – Only analyzes tables that have no existing statistics

- *gather stale* – Only reanalyzes tables that have a modification percentage greater than 10%. Modifications include inserts, updates, and deletes.

- *gather auto* – Reanalyzes objects that currently have no statistics and objects with stale statistics. Using *gather auto* is like combining *gather stale* and *gather empty.*

Note that both *gather stale* and *gather auto* require monitoring. If the *alter table xxx monitoring* command is issued, Oracle tracks changed tables with the *dba_tab_modifications* view. This allows the DBA to see the exact number of inserts, updates, and deletes tracked since the last analysis of statistics.

The *estimate_percent* option

The *estimate_percent* argument is a new way to allow Oracle's *dbms_stats* to automatically estimate the best percentage of a segment to sample when gathering statistics:

```
estimate_percent => dbms_stats.auto_sample_size
```

The accuracy of the automatic statistics sampling can be verified by looking at the *dba_tables* SAMPLE_SIZE column. It is interesting to note that Oracle chooses between 5 and 20 percent for a sample size when using automatic sampling. Better quality statistics means better decisions by the CBO.

The *method_opt* option

The *method_opt* parameter with *dbms_stats* is very useful for refreshing statistics when the table and index data change. The *method_opt* parameter is also very useful for determining which columns require histograms.

In some cases, the distribution of values within an index will effect the CBOs decision to use an index versus perform a full-table scan. This happens when a *where* clause has a disproportional amount of values, making a full-table scan cheaper than index access.

Oracle histograms statistics can be created when a highly skewed index exists, where some values have a disproportional number of rows. In the real world, this is quite rare, and one of the most common mistakes with the CBO is the unnecessary introduction of histograms in the CBO statistics. As a general rule, histograms are used when a column's values warrant a change to the execution plan.

To aid in intelligent histogram generation, Oracle uses the *method_opt* parameter of *dbms_stats*. There are also important new options within the *method_opt* clause, namely *skewonly*, *repeat* and *auto*:

```
method_opt=>'for all indexed columns size skewonly'
method_opt=>'for all columns size repeat'
method_opt=>'for columns size auto'
```

Parallel collection

Oracle allows for parallelism when collecting CBO statistics, which can greatly speed up the time required to collect statistics. A parallel statistics collection requires an SMP server with multiple CPUs.

Better execution speed

The *dbms_stats* utility is a great way to improve SQL execution speed. By using *dbms_stats* to collect top-quality statistics, the CBO will usually make an intelligent decision about the fastest way to execute any SQL query. The *dbms_stats* utility continues to improve and the exciting new features of automatic sample size and automatic histogram generation greatly simplify the job of the Oracle professional.

Gathering Data Dictionary Statistics

A new DBA task in Oracle Database 10g is to generate statistics on data dictionary objects contained in the SYS schema. The stored procedures *dbms_stats.gather_database_stats* and *dbms_stats.gather_schema_stats* can be used to gather the SYS schema stats. The following is an example of using *dbms_stats.gather_schema_stats* to gather data dictionary statistics:

```
EXEC dbms_stats.gather_schema_stats ('SYS');
```

It is a good idea to gather data dictionary statistics on a regular basis. Once per week should be sufficient on a database with average activity.

Gathering Fixed Table Statistics

Many of the Oracle data dictionary objects are called fixed tables because the DBA generally cannot modify them. In fact, although some of the data dictionary objects can be modified, this should never be done.

The procedures *dbms_stats.gather_database_stats* and *dbms_stats.gather_schema_stats* offer the *gather_fixed* parameter. When set to TRUE the *gather_fixed* parameter will cause fixed table statistics to be gathered along with regular database statistics. The following is an example of the collection of data dictionary stats and also the collection of fixed table statistics:

```
EXEC dbms_stats.gather_schema_stats ('SYS', gather_fixed=>TRUE);
```

Scheduling statistics collection

Determining when to collect statistics is not as easy as it seems. If a table is created, and then statistics are gathered on it, are those statistics really good? If the table is going to be populated with lots of data at a later time, then the statistics created when the table was first created will probably be no good. A table with a million rows will often generate a very different plan than a table with just 10.

If tables are static, then they probably only need to be analyzed when they change. If tables are dynamic, then a reoccurring analyze operation is probably the best thing to do. Analyzing dynamic tables once a day is far from unusual.

Sometimes there may be a need for user defined statistics in order to get good performance from new tables. Although this is fairly rare and is considered an advanced DBA topic, creating user defined statistics is possible.

Automatic Collection of Statistics

Oracle Database 10g actually automates the collection of database statistics out of the box. When an Oracle database is

---

created, a job will be scheduled that will generate the database statistics. System statistics, however, are not collected by the automatic statistics gathering mechanism.

The automated statistics collection job can be disabled using the *dbms_scheduler.disable* procedure as seen here:

```
EXEC dbms_scheduler.disable('GATHER_STATS_JOB');
```

The job can be re-enable using the *dbms_scheduler.enable* procedure as seen here:

```
EXEC dbms_scheduler.enable('GATHER_STATS_JOB');
```

Type the following string into the Google search engine to find more information: **bc oracle automatic cbo**

Administering Oracle Indexes

Tables can get quite big. Experienced DBA can be charged with managing databases with tables that are hundreds of Gigabytes in size, which is very big indeed! Big tables typically have a large number of rows in them. Imagine how long it might take to search through 500 million rows of a 200 Gigabyte table for one employee record. It could take a *very* long time.

One way to make accessing table data faster is to create an index on that table. Indexes are very common; there is an index at the end of this book. To learn more about a topic covered in this book, the reader can go to the end of the book, look in the index, and find which page to read for information on that topic. Without this index, finding a topic would be more difficult. Now imagine how long it would take to find every instance of the word "the" in the book.

By default Oracle uses B*Tree indexes. These indexes work very much the same way as the index in the back of this book. An index is built on one or more columns in the table. Those column values are stored in the index. Consider this scenario. An index is created on the EMPLOYEE_ID column. The index would have 500 million EMPLOYEE_ID values. Also in that index, with each EMPLOYEE_ID, is an address that tells Oracle exactly where that EMPLOYEE_ID is located in the table. This address is called the ROWID. The ROWID is like a home address, it identifies one and only one row in a table. Hence, armed with the column value, and the ROWID, Oracle can quickly find the rows that have the value being sought.

To find EMPLOYEE_ID 5555, part of the index might look like this:

COLUMN VALUE	ROWID
5551	AAAL+ZAAEAAAAMOAGa
5552	AAAL+ZAAEAAAAMOAGb
5553	AAAL+ZAAEAAAAMOAGc
5554	AAAL+ZAAEAAAAMOAGd
5555	AAAL+ZAAEAAAAMOAGe
5556	AAAL+ZAAEAAAAMOAGf
5556	AAAL+ZAAEAAAAMOAGg

Table 4.3: *Example index*

Oracle indexes are built so Oracle can very quickly find the column value entries that are being sought after. In this scenario, Oracle will then very quickly find the index entry for 5555, and read the associated ROWID. Based on the ROWID, it knows exactly where the row is in the table, and it will go read it.

The column values are sorted in the index. This makes looking for specific values or a range of values very fast. For example, to find all column values between 5553 and 5556, index reading would begin at 5553 and end after 5556. That makes for very quick lookups of a range of values. Queries like this can take advantage of these types of range scans:

```
SELECT empid, sal FROM emp WHERE empid BETWEEN 5553 AND 5556;
```

Also, since the column values are sorted, Oracle may not need to perform a sort operation. A query like the one that follows will require a sort if there is no index. However, since there is an index on the EMPID column, in many cases, Oracle will not need to do a sort as long as it uses that index to get the data that is needed.

```
SELECT empid, sal FROM emp WHERE empid BETWEEN 5553 AND 5556 ORDER
BY empid;
```

Oracle sometimes creates indexes automatically. When a primary key constraint is defined, Oracle will create an index. When a unique constraint is defined, Oracle will also create an index.

⌨ Type the following string into the Google search engine to find more information: **bc oracle index**

The default index type that Oracle uses is B*Tree indexes. A picture of the index makes it look like an upside down tree. At this point, it is not important that to know how a B*Tree index really works, just remember that they are very fast and efficient for many kinds of queries. If queries are going to look at only a certain amount of table data, indexes can improve the speed of the queries several fold. Here is a graphic of a B*Tree Index.

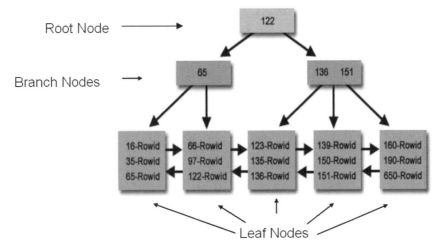

Figure 4.1: *B*Tree Index*

In the graphic of the B*Tree index, Oracle starts from the top box called the root node, and works its way past the intermediate branch nodes down to the bottom boxes, called the leaf nodes, to find the data. The root node points to the correct branch node to go to, which then points to the correct leaf node based on the data value being sought.

For example, to find the value of 64 in the B*Tree graphic in Figure 4.1, the root node points to the left branch node because it contains all values up to 122. This branch node then points to the left most leaf node because the left most lead node contains all values up to 65. The ROWID for record 65 is located there. Oracle will then take that ROWID and read the correct row in the table.

Usually this is a very fast and efficient way to get to specific data elements. It can also be a very expensive process since it took 4 I/O's to get just one record out of the table. This breaks down to 3 index I/O's and 1 table I/O. Therefore, indexes are not always the best way to get at table data. A study of Oracle Performance

Tuning will provide a better understanding of when indexes are good and when they are bad. Since this book is about being a DBA and managing the database, that discussion will have to wait until another day.

Oracle can use other kinds of indexes, such as index organized tables, function based indexes, and indexed clusters. These are slightly more advanced topics and best saved for another book. In this book, B*Tree indexes will be the main focus. Also, Oracle offers advanced functionality with indexes such as partitioning and key compression. This book is designed to get the aspiring DBA through the basics first. Once that is accomplished and the DBA has gained some comfort with them, these more complex index options can be explored in more detail later.

Creating Indexes

Once the decision has been made than an index is needed, the CREATE INDEX command is used. The command is pretty straightforward as seen in this example:

```
CREATE INDEX ix_emp_01 ON emp (deptno) TABLESPACE index_tbs;
```

This statement creates an index called IX_EMP_01. This index is built on the DEPTNO column of the EMP table. The tablespace that the index should be created in is also defined using the TABLESPACE keyword. In this case, it was created in the INDEX_TBS tablespace.

Indexes can be created on multiple columns in a table. What if an index needed to be created on the EMP table columns EMPNO and DEPTNO? A concatenated index would be used and it is created this way:

```
CREATE INDEX ix_emp_01 ON emp (empno, deptno) TABLESPACE index_tbs;
```

Altering Indexes

If indexes are created, there may be times that attributes of that index need to be changed, for instance, where it is stored. Also, sometimes an index needs to be rebuilt to help with performance. For cases like these, the ALTER INDEX command is used. The following is an example of the use of the ALTER INDEX command:

```
ALTER INDEX ix_emp_01 REBUILD TABLESPACE new_index;
```

In this example, the ALTER INDEX command is used to rebuild an index. The REBUILD keyword is what tells Oracle to rebuild the index. The TABLESPACE keyword followed by a tablespace name is used to instruct Oracle as to where to recreate the rebuilt index. By default Oracle will create the rebuilt index in the same tablespace.

The ALTER INDEX command using the RENAME TO keyword allows a tablespace to be renamed as seen in this example:

```
ALTER INDEX ix_emp_01 RENAME TO ix_emp_01_old;
```

In this case, the ix_emp_01 index is renamed to ix_emp_01_old. All of the data dictionary entries will be changed by Oracle to reflect the new name. Indexes and the data dictionary will be covered shortly.

Dropping Indexes

Sometimes what is created must be destroyed. When it is time to remove an index, the DROP INDEX command is what is needed. The drop index command is pretty straight forward as seen in the following example:

```
DROP INDEX ix_emp_01_old;
```

Special Non-Tree Indexes

Oracle includes many indexing algorithms that dramatically increase the speed with which Oracle queries are serviced. This section explores the internals of Oracle indexing; reviews the standard B*Tree index, bitmap indexes, function-based indexes, and index-organized tables (IOTs); and demonstrates how these indexes may dramatically increase the speed of Oracle SQL queries.

Oracle uses indexes to avoid the need for large-table, full-table scans and disk sorts, which are required when the SQL optimizer cannot find an efficient way to service the SQL query. This review will begin with the standard Oracle b-tree index methodologies.

While b-tree indexes are great for simple queries, they are not very good for the following situations:

- **Low-cardinality columns:** Columns with less than 200 distinct values do not have the selectivity required in order to benefit from standard b-tree index structures.

- **SQL functions:** B-tree indexes are not able to support SQL queries using Oracle's built-in functions.

    Oracle provides a variety of built-in functions that allow SQL statements to query on a piece of an indexed column or on any one of a number of transformations against the indexed column.

Prior to Oracle9i, the Oracle SQL optimizer had to perform time-consuming long-table, full-table scans due to these shortcomings. Consequently, it was no surprise when Oracle introduced more robust types of indexing structures.

Bitmapped indexes

Oracle bitmap indexes are very different from standard B*Ttree indexes. In bitmap structures, a two-dimensional array is created with one column for every row in the table being indexed. Each column represents a distinct value within the bitmapped index. This two-dimensional array represents each value within the index multiplied by the number of rows in the table. At row retrieval time, Oracle decompresses the bitmap into the RAM data buffers so it can be rapidly scanned for matching values. These matching values are delivered to Oracle in the form of a Row-ID list, and these Row-ID values may directly access the required information.

⬚ Type the following string into the Google search engine to find more information: **bc oracle bitmap**.

The real benefit of bitmapped indexing occurs when one table includes multiple bitmapped indexes. Each individual column may have low cardinality. The creation of multiple bitmapped indexes provides a very powerful method for rapidly answering difficult SQL queries.

For example, assume there is a motor vehicle database with numerous low-cardinality columns such as CAR_COLOR, CAR_MAKE, CAR_MODEL, and CAR_YEAR. Each column contains less than 100 distinct values by themselves and a B*Tree index would be fairly useless in a database of 20 million vehicles. However, combining these indexes together in a query can provide blistering response times a lot faster than the traditional method of reading each one of the 20 million rows in the base table. This example queries the motor vehicle database for blue Toyota Corollas manufactured in 1981:

```
select
   license_plat_nbr
from
   vehicle
```

```
where
   color = 'blue'
and
   make = 'toyota'
and
   year = 1981;
```

Oracle uses a specialized optimizer method called a bitmapped index merge to service this query. In a bitmapped index merge, each Row ID (RID) list is built independently by using the bitmaps. A special merge routine is used in order to compare the RID lists and find the intersecting values.

Using this methodology, Oracle can provide sub-second response time when working against multiple low-cardinality columns:

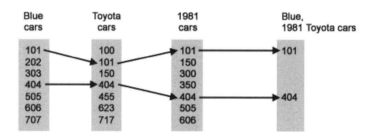

Figure 4.2: *Bitmapped index merge*

Function-based indexes

One important advance in Oracle indexing is function-based indexing. Function-based indexes allow for creation of indexes on expressions, internal functions, and user-written functions in PL/SQL and Java. Function-based indexes ensure that the Oracle designer is able to use an index for a query. Prior to Oracle8, the use of a built-in function would not be able to match the performance of an index. Consequently, Oracle would perform the dreaded full-table scan. Examples of SQL with function-based queries might include the following:

```
Select * from customer where substr(cust_name,1,4) = 'BURL';
Select * from customer where to_char(order_date,'MM') = '01;
Select * from customer where upper(cust_name) = 'JONES';
Select * from customer where initcap(first_name) = 'Mike';
```

Oracle always interrogates the *where* clause of the SQL statement to see if a matching index exists. By using function-based indexes, the Oracle designer can create a matching index that exactly matches the predicates within the SQL where clause. This ensures that the query is retrieved with a minimal amount of disk I/O and at the fastest possible speed.

🖳 Type the following string into the Google search engine to find more information: **bc oracle function based indexes**.

Index Organized Tables

Oracle recognized that a table with an index built on every column did not require table rows to exist! In other words, Oracle recognized that by using a special table-access method called an index fast full scan, the index could be queried without actually touching the data itself.

Oracle codified this idea with its use of index organized table (IOT) structure. When using an IOT, Oracle does not create the actual table but instead keeps all of the required information inside the Oracle index.

At query time, the Oracle SQL optimizer recognizes that all of the values necessary to service the query exist within the index tree, at which time the Oracle cost-based optimizer has a choice of either reading through the index tree nodes to pull the information in sorted order or invoke an index fast full scan, which will read the table in the same fashion as a full table scan, using sequential prefetch, as defined by the *db_file_multiblock_read_count* parameter.

The multiblock read facility allows Oracle to very quickly scan index blocks in linear order, quickly reading every block within the index tablespace. Here is an example of the syntax to create an IOT.

```
CREATE TABLE emp_iot (
    emp_id number,
    ename varchar2(20),
    sal number(9,2),
    deptno number,
    CONSTRAINT pk_emp_iot_index PRIMARY KEY (emp_id) )
ORGANIZATION index
TABLESPACE spc_demo_ts_01
PCTHRESHOLD 20 INCLUDING ename;
```

⌨ Type the following string into the Google search engine to find more information: **bc oracle iot**.

Oracle index dictionary views

A DBA needs to manage indexes. This includes knowing who owns the index, what tablespace the index is in, and what columns for which the index is being built. The following data dictionary views are used for these purposes:

- *dba_indexes, all_indexes, user_indexes*

- *dba_ind_columns, all_ind_columns, user_ind_columns*

There is an almost infinite number of ways that details can be queried from the *dba_indexes* view. For example, here is a simple query to show its tables and freelists:

```
col c1 heading 'Table|Name'       format a20
col c2 heading 'Table|Freelists'  format 99
col c3 heading 'Index|Name'       format a20
col c4 heading 'Index|Freelists'  format 99

select distinct
    t.table_name   c1,
    t.freelists    c2,
    index_name     c3,
    i.freelists    c4
from
    dba_tables     t,
```

```
   dba_indexes   i
where
   t.table_name = i.table_name
and
   i.index_name = 'IDX_EVENTCASE_STATUS_OVERAGE'
```

⌨ Type the following string into the Google search engine to find more information: **bc oracle index scripts**.

Generating Indexes on Statistics

The importance of statistics on tables and indexes was covered earlier in this Chapter. Statistics have to be generated in such a way that both the table and indexes will have statistics collected. Of course, with the creation of a new index comes the need to generate statistics for that new index.

Fortunately, Oracle Database 10g realizes how important indexes are, and will actually create them when it creates an index. Oracle will also regenerate statistics on an index when it is rebuilt. Hence, for the most part, the DBA doesn't need to worry about generating statistics on just indexes in Oracle Database 10g.

Administering Oracle Views

As a DBA, one of the types of objects that will need to be managed will be views. This section will introduce Oracle view constructs. Following the introduction to views, the benefits and downsides of views in Oracle will be presented.

Inside Oracle Views

A view is simply the representation of an SQL statement that is stored in memory so that it can easily be re-used. For example, if the following query if frequently issued:

```
SELECT empid FROM emp;
```

The DBA may want to make this a view. The reality is that a view for a statement this simple would probably never be created, but for demonstration purposes, this is an easy example.

To create a view, use the CREATE VIEW command as shown in the following example:

```
CREATE VIEW view_emp
AS
SELECT empid FROM emp;
```

This command creates a new view called VIEW_EMP. Note that this command does not result in anything being actually stored in the database at all except for a data dictionary entry that defines this view. This means that every time this view is queried, Oracle has to go out and execute the view and query the database data. The following is an example of how this view can be queried:

```
SELECT * FROM view_emp WHERE empid BETWEEN 500 AND 1000;
```

Oracle will transform the query into the following:

```
SELECT * FROM (select empid from emp) WHERE empid BETWEEN 500 AND
1000;
```

Benefits of Oracle Views

Oracle views offer some compelling benefits. These include:

- **Commonality of code being used.** Since a view is based on one common set of SQL, this means that when it is called it is less likely to require parsing. This is because the basic underlying SQL that is called is always the same. However, since additional *where* clauses can be included when calling a view, bind variables still need to be used. Additional *where* clauses without a bind variable can still cause a hard parse!

- **Security.** Views have long been used to hide the tables that actually contain the data being queried. Also, views can be used to restrict the columns that a given user has access to. Using views for security on less complex databases is probably not a bad thing. As databases become more complex, this solution becomes harder to scale and other solutions will be needed.

- **Predicate pushing.** Oracle supports pushing of predicates into a given view. The following example assumes a set of layered views exists:

```
-- View One
CREATE VIEW vw_layer_one
AS SELECT * FROM emp;

-- view two
CREATE VIEW vw_layer_two_dept_100
AS SELECT * FROM vw_layer_one
WHERE deptno=100;
```

Then assume the following query is issued:

```
SELECT * FROM vw_layer_two_dept_100
WHERE empid=100;
```

The predicate in this statement is the *where empid=100* statement. There may be one of tens or even hundreds of predicates. Oracle will, in many cases, push those predicates down into the views being called. Thus, Oracle will transform the VW_LAYER_ONE view into a SQL statement that looks like this:

```
CREATE VIEW vw_layer_one
AS SELECT * FROM emp
WHERE deptno=100
AND empid=100;
```

Note that both the predicate from view two (*where deptno=100*) and the predicate from the SQL statement being executed (*where empid=100*) are pushed down into the final view that is executed. This can have significant performance benefits because now the bottom view can possibly use an index if one exists on *deptno* and/or *empid*.

Predicate pushing has a number of restrictions that are beyond the scope of this book, but they can be found in the Oracle documentation. Also, any predicate pushing may result in a hard parse of the underlying SQL that is executed. Hence, it is important to make sure bind variables are used instead of literals in SQL code calling views. Thus, our SQL should look something like this instead for best performance:

```
SELECT * FROM vw_layer_two_dept_100
WHERE empid=:b100;
```

The downside to using Views

Views are very handy, but they can get badly abused, which is a shame. It is possible to have a view that returns 50 columns, and has 40 predicates used to return just two or three columns that could easily have been retrieved from a simple SQL query. This is clearly a case of view abuse, and can lead to badly performing views.

Stacked views can also mask performance problems. Again, they can result in innumerable columns being returned when all that is really needed is a few of those columns. Also, predicate pushing tends to break down as more and more views are stacked. Before starting to stack views, the DBA should carefully review the rules for predicate pushing in the Oracle documentation. They are rather long and involved!

Administering Oracle Constraints

Oracle constraints are critical to the scalability, flexibility and integrity of database data. Constraints apply specific rules to data, ensuring the data conforms to the requirements defined. There are a number of different kinds of constraints that the DBA should be concerned with. These are:

- CHECK
- NOT NULL
- PRIMARY KEY
- UNIQUE
- FOREIGN KEY

Each of these will be covered in a little more detail in the following sections.

Check Constraints

CHECK constraints validate that values in a given column meet a specific criteria. For example, a check constraint could be created on a varchar2 column so it can only contain the values T or F as in the following example:

```
Create table my_status
( status_id      NUMBER      PRIMARY KEY,
  person_id      NUMBER      NOT NULL,
  active_record VARCHAR2(1) NOT NULL
  CHECK (UPPER(active_record)='T' or
         UPPER(active_record)='F'),
  person_ssn    VARCHAR2(20) CONSTRAINT un_person_ssn UNIQUE
);
```

In this example, a table is created called MY_STATUS using the CREATE TABLE command. The CONSTRAINT keyword indicates that a constraint will be defined. This particular example is known as an in-line constraint because the constraint is being defined in the same line as the column being defined.

To add a CHECK CONSTRAINT to a table after the fact, simply use the ALTER TABLE command. Here is an example:

```
ALTER TABLE my_status ADD (CONSTRAINT ck_stats_01
  CHECK (UPPER(active_record)='T' or
         UPPER(active_record)='F') );
```

NOT NULL Constraints

NOT NULL constraints are in-line constraints that indicate that a column can not contain NULL values. The previous example of the creation of the MY_STATUS table contained two examples of NOT NULL constraints being defined. For example, the PERSON_ID column is defined as NOT NULL in that example.

To add a NOT NULL constraint to a table after the fact, simply use the ALTER TABLE command as shown in this example:

```
ALTER TABLE my_status MODIFY ( person_id NOT NULL);
```

PRIMARY KEY Constraints

PRIMARY KEY constraints define a column or series of columns that uniquely identify a given row in a table. Defining a primary key on a table is optional and there can only be a single primary key on a table. A PRIMARY KEY constraint can consist of one or as many as 32 columns. Any column that is defined as a primary key column is automatically set with a NOT NULL status.

The previous example of the creation of the MY_STATUS table included the definition of the STATUS_ID column as the primary key of that table by using the PRIMARY KEY keyword.

To PRIMARY KEY constraint a table after the fact, simply use the ALTER TABLE command.

```
ALTER TABLE my_status ADD CONSTRAINT pk_my_status
PRIMARY KEY (status_id);
```

UNIQUE Constraints

UNIQUE constraints are like alternative PRIMARY KEY constraints. A UNIQUE constraint defines a column, or series of columns, that must be unique. A number of UNIQUE constraints can be defined and the columns can have NULL values in them, unlike a column that belongs to a PRIMARY KEY constraint. To add UNIQUE key constraints to a table after the fact, simply use the ALTER TABLE command.

```
ALTER TABLE my_status ADD CONSTRAINT uk_my_status
UNIQUE (status_id, person_id);
```

FOREIGN KEY Constraints

A FOREIGN KEY constraint is used to enforce a relationship between two tables. As an example, take the case of two tables, ITEM and PART. These tables have a relationship because an item can have none, one, or many parts. FOREIGN KEY constraints help to enforce that relationship. In the DBA world, diagrams called Entity Relationship Diagrams (ERD) are used to show visually how tables relate. Here is an ERD that shows how the ITEM and PART tables relate.

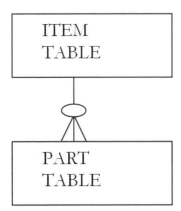

Figure 4.3: *Entity Relationship Diagram*

The ITEM and PART tables are diagramed in two boxes. There is a line between the two. The two lines from the PART table to the main line between the ITEM and PART tables are called crow's feet. Crow's feet indicate a one-to-many relationship between the tables.

In the diagram above, there is a one-to-many relationship between the ITEM and PART tables. An item may have no parts assigned to build it, perhaps it is new and in development, or it may have one or many parts that go into building the part. Notice the circle at the top of the crow's feet. Since it is not filled in, that indicates that there may not be any parts in the PART table. If the circle was darkened, this would indicate that there must be at least one part associated with each item.

So, how does this relate to FOREIGN KEY constraints? Well, FOREIGN KEY constraints help to enforce the type of relationship between tables. This example demonstrates how to create the ITEM and PART table. In the process of doing so, a foreign key relationship will be created between the two:

```
CREATE TABLE part(
Part_no    NUMBER PRIMARY KEY,
Part_desc VARCHAR2(200) NOT NULL );

CREATE TABLE item (
Item_no    NUMBER,
Part_no    NUMBER,
Item_desc varchar2 (200) NOT NULL,
CONSTRAINT fk_item_part FOREIGN KEY (part_no) REFERENCES PART
(part_no),
CONSTRAINT pk_item PRIMARY  KEY (item_no, part_no) );
```

In this example, focus on the creation of the ITEM table. The primary key is defined as an out of line primary key. This is because it is a composite primary key and composite primary keys have to be defined out of line.

Now, look at the foreign key definition. FOREIGN KEY constraints are defined as out of line constraints as shown in the example. The following is a snippet of the command that was used:

```
CONSTRAINT fk_item_part FOREIGN KEY (part_no) REFERENCES part
(part_no);
```

The example starts out using the CONSTRAINT keyword. This tells Oracle that a constraint is being defined. Then, the constraint is named *fk_item_part*. Constraint names have to be unique for each table and can be no more than 30 characters in length. Then the FOREIGN KEY keyword is used to indicate that a foreign key constraint is being defined. Next, the column in the table being created that this foreign key belongs to is defined.

The REFERENCES keyword is used next to define the table and column that this foreign key references. The referenced table is the PART table. Finally, the column in the PART table that is being referenced is defined as PART_NO.

The bottom line is that now a part cannot be added to the ITEM table unless it is listed in the PART table. This ensures data integrity is maintained. To add FOREIGN KEY constraints to a table after the fact, simply use the ALTER TABLE command as seen here:

```
ALTER TABLE my_status ADD CONSTRAINT fk_my_status
FOREIGN KEY (part_no) REFERENCES part (part_no);
```

Conclusion

There is no mystery behind Oracle. Though there are many components that bring it all together, if it is boiled down to the basics, what is left is something that is easy to grasp.

Tables hold our data, indexes make it easy to find, and constraints ensure data integrity. DBA's all start with these basic elements.

The main points of this chapter include:

- Oracle tables are the basic structure for storing data.

- Tables are logical structures that consist of one-or-more columns.

- Table columns can have many datatypes, including character, number, date and many others.

- Tables are placed into a tablespace when they are created.

- Indexes can be created on tables to speed-up rows access by SQL statements.

- Statistics must be collected periodically to provide the SQL optimizer with information about the number of rows in the table, the distribution of columns, etc.

The next chapter will begin an exploration of Oracle users and see how Oracle has powerful tools to manage security. Properly configured, Oracle is can be a virtually unbreakable database.

Oracle Users and Security

Now that methods for creating Objects like tables and indexes have been presented, it is time to create a few users so that someone can actually use those objects. Once there are users logging onto the database and actually using it, it will be necessary to ensure the data is secure from those who should not be able to see it or change anything.

In this chapter, user administration will be covered first, followed by database security related topics such as grants, roles and synonyms.

Administration of Oracle Users

One of the more common tasks of the DBA is the creation of the database user. Each database user is assigned a unique username. Users will log into the database using that username, and having logged in, users can issue various database SQL statements to create objects, query objects and manage the database.

This section will cover the creation of users with the CREATE USER command. It will also cover using the ALTER USER command to administer users and finally using the DROP USER command to drop users from the database.

Creating Users

The CREATE USER command is used to create database user accounts. When creating a user account with the CREATE USER command the DBA can:

- Define the user name

- Define the password associated with the database user

- Define the default tablespace for the user

- Define the temporary tablespace for the user

- Allocate space quotas to various tablespaces to the user.

- Assign attributes to the user account

Here is an example of the use of the CREATE USER command:

```
CREATE USER myuser IDENTIFIED BY password
DEFAULT TABLESPACE users
TEMPORARY TABLESPACE temp
QUOTA UNLIMITED ON users
QUOTA 100M ON my_data;
```

In this example, the CREATE USER command is used to create a user called MYUSER. The IDENTIFIED BY clause is used to define the password, which is password in this case. Next the DEFAULT TABLESPACE keyword is used to define the location of the default tablespace, which is USERS. The TEMPORARY TABLESPACE keyword defines the temporary tablespace that will be assigned to the user, which in this scenario is the TEMP tablespace.

How much space a user can take up in a tablespace can be controlled through the use of quotas. In the previous example quotas were defined on two different tablespaces using the QUOTA keyword. First, an unlimited quota is granted to MYUSER on the USERS tablespace using the QUOTA UNLIMITED keywords. Second, MYUSER is limited to a 100

Megabyte quota on the MY_DATA tablespace using the QUOTA 100M keywords. In this example, M means Megabyte.

The following codes can be used to represent different space allocation types:

CODE	SPACE ALLOCATION TYPE
K	Kilobytes (1,000 bytes)
M	Megabytes (1,000,000 bytes)
G	Gigabytes (1,000,000,000 bytes) – Only available in Oracle Database 10g.

Table 5.1: *Space allocation types*

Administering Oracle Users

When creating users, the DBA needs to be able to do things like change a user's password and other various attributes. The ALTER USER command is used for these tasks. Here are some examples of the uses of the ALTER USER command in action:

```
ALTER USER myuser IDENTIFIED BY new_password;

ALTER USER myuser
DEFAULT TABLESPACE users TEMPORARY TABLESPACE temp
QUOTA 100M ON users QUOTA 0 ON my_data;

ALTER USER myuser ACCOUNT LOCK;
ALTER USER myuser ACCOUNT UNLOCK;
ALTER USER myuser PASSWORD EXPIRE;
```

In the first example, the password of the *myuser* user was changed. In the next example the default and temporary tablespace settings for the *myuser* user were altered, and the quotas on two different tablespaces were also changed. The next two examples lock the *myuser* account, and then unlock the *myuser* account.

The final example uses EXPIRE to cause the password of the *myuser* account to expire, which will force the user to change their password the next time they log in.

Dropping Users

If the DBA is going to create users, he or she better be able to remove them. The DROP USER command performs this action. The command is as simple as DROP USER followed by the user name. If the user owns objects, for example, if the user created a table and an index using their user ID, then the CASCADE parameter will need to be added, as seen in the following example:

```
DROP USER myuser CASCADE;
```

Oracle Users and Security

Once a user has been created, that user may need to be able to do something in a database. A created user has no privileges, for example, they can not even connect to the database. This section will address this problem by assigning users the privileges they need to actually get some work done. System privileges will be addressed first, followed by object privileges. After that, information will be presented on how roles can be used to make user administration much easier.

System Privileges

System privileges allow the user to perform system level activities. This might include such things as being able to actually connect to the system, or it might include the ability to do things like create objects in schemas other than their own schema. The next sections cover the GRANT command, which can be used to grant system privileges. Also, the REVOKE command will be covered, which can be used to revoke privileges from users.

🖧 Type the following string into the Google search engine to find more information: **bc oracle system privileges**.

Granting System Level Privileges

The GRANT command is used to grant system level privileges. System level privileges are those privileges that are needed to actually do something on the system. For example, a user would be granted system level privileges so they can:

- Connect to the database (CREATE SESSION)

- Create objects (CREATE TABLE, CREATE INDEX)

- Perform DBA activities, like backup the database (SYSDBA, SYSOPER)

- Alter session related parameters (ALTER SESSION)

Basically, even if a user account is created, it will not be able to do anything until a basic set of privileges has been assigned. Typically the DBA would always GRANT the CREATE SESSION privilege so that the user can connect to the database.

The GRANT command is pretty simple to use, all that needs to be known is what privilege to grant and to whom that privilege should be granted. For example, for the user to be able to create an index, that user would be granted the CREATE INDEX privilege with the GRANT command as shown in the following example:

```
GRANT CREATE INDEX TO RAMPANT;
```

There are a number of different privileges that can be assigned to a given user. In fact, there are way too many to list here. A list of the different privileges that can be assigned to a given user can be found in the Oracle SQL Reference Guide under the GRANT command documentation.

Multiple privileges can also be granted in the same GRANT command by simply separating the privileges by a comma as shown in the following example:

```
GRANT CREATE INDEX, SELECT ANY TABLE TO RAMPANT;
```

Notice the use of the word ANY, as in SELECT ANY TABLE. Using the ANY keyword in reference to a system privilege means that the user can perform the privilege on any objects owned by any user except for SYS. By default, if a user is granted a privilege, they cannot assign that privilege to others. That privilege cannot be granted or revoked to or from anyone else. Sometime the DBA may want to grant privileges to users and have them be able to grant those privileges to other users. When this is the case, the WITH ADMIN keyword is included in the GRANT command. When this keyword is used, it will allow the user granted the privilege to grant that privilege to other users. Here is an example of the usage of the WITH ADMIN OPTION keyword.

```
GRANT CREATE INDEX TO RAMPANT WITH ADMIN OPTION;
```

Revoking System Level Privileges

The REVOKE command is used to revoke system level privileges that were previously granted with the GRANT command. Simply enter the privilege to revoke in the body of the REVOKE command as seen in the following example:

```
REVOKE CREATE INDEX FROM RAMPANT;
```

To be able to revoke a privilege from another user that privilege must have been granted to the user who is doing the revoking with the ADMIN OPTION. This was demonstrated earlier in the section. Revoking system level privileges will only impact the user from which the privileges are being revoked. Any user that was granted system privileges by that user will still continue to have those privileges.

All privileges can be revoked from a user with the ALL PRIVILEGES option of the REVOKE command, as seen in the following example:

```
REVOKE ALL PRIVILEGES FROM RAMPANT;
```

Object Privileges

Once a user has been created been granted system privileges, they will start creating objects. Undoubtedly, the DBA will also be creating objects. Once objects are created, only the user who created those objects will be able to actually do anything with them. This is not particularly useful since their User ID and password should not be given to everyone in the world. Oracle utilizes the GRANT and REVOKE commands to enable others users to gain access to objects in the database. These commands will be explored in more detail in the following sections.

Granting Object Level Privileges

In order to allow others to access a user's objects, the GRANT command can be utilized. Yes, the very same GRANT command used to grant system privileges can be used to allow different kinds of access to a user's objects. For example, the user TOM can be granted access to the EMP table in the SCOTT account (or schema) with this command:

```
GRANT SELECT ON emp TO scott;
```

Only the schema that owns the object can grant privileges to that object unless the WITH GRANT OPTION is included in the command. The WITH GRANT OPTION allows the user being assigned the privilege the ability to grant that privilege to other users. Here is an example of the use of the WITH GRANT OPTION:

```
GRANT SELECT ON emp TO scott WITH GRANT OPTION
```

Revoking Object Level Privileges

When a user should no longer have access rights to an object, the REVOKE command is used to remove those rights as seen in the following example:

```
REVOKE SELECT on emp FROM scott;
```

There is one major difference in the revocation of object privileges and system privileges. With objects, a privilege is revoked from a user who had been granted it with the WITH GRANT OPTION, Oracle acts a bit different. In this case, the revoke operation will affect not only the user from whom the privileges are being revoked, but all other users to whom that user had granted privileges will have those privileges revoked as well. Hence, be careful revoking object privileges as it is an easy way to end up breaking something!

Synonyms

A synonym allows a pointer to be created to an object that exists somewhere else. Synonyms are needed when a user is logged into Oracle because Oracle looks for all objects being queried in that user's schema or account. If the objects are not there, it will generate an error indicating that they do not exist. For example, assume a query such as SELECT * FROM emp is issued from the RAMPANT schema and the emp table is not there. The following error is generated:

```
SQL> select * from emp;
select * from emp
               *
ERROR at line 1:
ORA-00942: table or view does not exist
```

The results of the query show why this is a problem:

```
SQL> select table_name from user_tables where table_name='EMP';

no rows selected
```

Clearly there is no EMP table, which can be a problem. Well, the truth is that there is an EMP table in the database, it is just owned by a user called SCOTT as can be seen in the following query:

```
SQL> select owner, table_name from dba_tables where
table_name='EMP';

OWNER                          TABLE_NAME
------------------------------ ------------------------
SCOTT                          EMP
```

Since the table is in the SCOTT schema, and assuming the user has been granted SELECT privileges to that table, he can query the table this way:

```
SQL> select * from scott.emp;

EMPNO ENAME      JOB        MGR  HIREDATE      SAL   COMM   DEPTNO
----- ---------- --------- ----- --------- -------- ------- --------
 3333 R Freeman  BOSS            24-AUG-05
 7369 SMITH      CLERK      7902 24-AUG-05      800               20
 7499 ALLEN      SALESMAN   7698 24-AUG-05     1600     300       30
 7521 WARD       SALESMAN   7698 24-AUG-05     1250     500       30
```

SCOTT was added to the beginning of the EMP table reference. This indicates that the query is intended to be executed against the EMP table in the SCOTT schema, and sure enough there is the table.

A user is an account that can be logged into. Every user has a schema, which is a virtual space for the user to create their objects. Consequently, the words Users and Schemas are often used interchangeably, making them Synonyms. However, it would be a bit of a pain to have to always prefix all SQL calls to the EMP table with SCOTT, so there must be an easier way. There is, the way is called synonyms. The following section covers the creation and removal of synonyms.

Creating Synonyms

A synonym is named and points to a specific object. For example, in the RAMPANT schema a private synonym can be created for SCOTT.EMP using the CREATE SYNONYM command:

```
SQL> CREATE SYNONYM emp FOR SCOTT.EMP;
```

Now, when the query is issued with just the EMP, removing the SCOTT, the results will be the data from the SCOTT.EMP table because Oracle will follow the synonym to the correct place as seen in the following example:

```
SQL> select * from emp;
EMPNO ENAME      JOB        MGR HIREDATE      SAL    COMM   DEPTNO
----- ---------- ---------- ----- --------- -------- ------- --------
 3333 R Freeman  BOSS           24-AUG-05
 7369 SMITH      CLERK      7902 24-AUG-05     800               20
 7499 ALLEN      SALESMAN   7698 24-AUG-05    1600    300        30
 7521 WARD       SALESMAN   7698 24-AUG-05    1250    500        30
```

This was a private synonym, which means that only the RAMPANT user can use the synonym. Public synonyms can be created using the CREATE PUBLIC SYNONYM command as seen in the following example:

```
SQL> CREATE PUBLIC SYNONYM emp FOR SCOTT.EMP;
```

Good DBA's try to avoid public synonyms. While they can make management of the database a bit easier, they also have associated security and performance issues. Hence, it's a best practice to not use them unless it is absolutely necessary.

A public and private synonym can be created with the same name. In fact, there can be a public and private synonym called EMP in the SCOTT schema as well as a table called EMP in the same schema. In cases where there are multiple synonyms and/or a table present, it can get confusing which object is being used. There is an order of precedence with regards to the use of synonyms and local objects. This order is:

- Local objects will always be accessed first.

- If a local object does not exist, the object with a private synonym will be accessed.

- If a private synonym does not exist or the object does not exist, then the public synonym will be used.

A synonym can be created for an object that does not exist, and an object with an associated synonym can be dropped without removing the synonym. This can cause all sorts of interesting problems for DBA's, so be careful.

Removing Synonyms

The DROP SYNONYM command is used to drop public and private synonyms. Here is an example of dropping a private synonym and a public synonym with the DROP SYNONYM command:

```
SQL> -- Drop public synony
SQL> DROP PUBLIC SYNONYM emp;

SQL> -- Drop private synonym
SQL> DROP SYNONYM emp;
```

Using Oracle Roles

Administration of large numbers of objects can be difficult. Roles allow the administration of objects to be localized. Roles are most helpful when large numbers of users will need the same system and object privileges.

Think of a role like a database user that nobody uses. The role is created using the CREATE ROLE command. Next, the role is granted all of the common privileges that users will require to perform their work, like the ability to select, insert, update, and delete data from various tables.

🖧 Type the following string into the Google search engine to find more information: **bc oracle security roles**.

Once the role is setup, the role needs to be granted to users and all the privileges will be transferred along with that grant. Later, additional privileges can be added to the role if required.

The CREATE ROLE command is used to create a role and then the role is granted to the user with the GRANT command as seen in this example:

```
SQL> Create role select_data_role;
SQL> Grant select on emp, dept, bonus to select_data_role;
```

The DBA can then grant that role to other users as in this case where the *select_data_role* is granted to RAMPANT. Once this is done, RAMPANT will be able to query the EMP, DEPT and BONUS tables in the SCOTT schema:

```
SQL> GRANT select_data_role TO RAMPANT;
```

Roles have some limitations. Object privileges granted through roles can not be used when writing PL/SQL code. When writing

PL/SQL code, direct grants to the objects in the database that the code is accessing must be used.

To revoke a role from a user, simply use the REVOKE command:

```
SQL> REVOKE select_data_role FROM RAMPANT;
```

Conclusion

This chapter has not only demonstrated how to create a user, but how to allow that user to perform different activities. Without users, a database would certainly perform well, because it would not be able to actually do anything.

With users, the database can be populated with plenty of objects and logins to interact with these objects. With privileges and roles, the DBA can be assured that no user has too much ability.

The main points of this chapter include:

- All Oracle objects (tables, indexes) are owned by users.

- By default, only the user who created a table may see the rows. To allow other users to see rows, the user must grant access privileges.

- Oracle has system privileges that allow global access rights.

- Oracle has object privileges that allow grants to specific tables.

- Any privilege can be removed with the REVOKE command.

Now it is time to dive into the internal Oracle database, the metadata, or data about the data that gives the DBA a powerful tool for administering the database.

The Oracle Data Dictionary and Dynamic Performance Views

CHAPTER

6

Managing Oracle requires the use of a number of Oracle supplied views. These views include the data dictionary and the dynamic performance views. Together these views allow the DBA to:

- Manage the database

- Tune the database

- Monitor the database

In this chapter, the data dictionary views will be covered first. The, information about the dynamic performance views available in Oracle Database 10g will be presented.

The Oracle Data Dictionary

At the heart of every Oracle database is the data dictionary. The data dictionary is generated when the database is first created. The next section covers the Oracle data dictionary. The topic will include:

- The purpose of the data dictionary

- The architecture of the data dictionary

- Uses of the data dictionary

The Purpose of the Data Dictionary

Metadata is data about data, or data that defines other data. The Oracle data dictionary is metadata about the database. For

158

Easy Oracle Jumpstart

example, when a table is created in Oracle, metadata about that table is stored in the data dictionary. Such things as column names, length, and other attributes are stored. Thus, the data dictionary contains a great volume of useful information about the database. Pretty much everything a DBA would want to know about their database is contained in the data dictionary in some form.

As a DBA then, it is easy to see why the data dictionary is so important. Since a DBA cannot possibly remember everything about a database, like the names of all the tables and columns, Oracle remembers this information. All the DBA needs to do is learn how to find that information. This process will be presented later in this book.

The Architecture of the Data Dictionary

The data dictionary is created when the Oracle database is created. It is owned by the SYS user, and is stored principally in the SYSTEM tablespace, though some components are stored in the SYSAUX tablespace in Oracle Database 10g.

The data dictionary is comprised of a number of tables and Oracle views. Oracle wants these tables to remain hands off, and unless the DBA is following a directive from Oracle Technical Support, it would be best to heed this advice.

Of course, the data dictionary would be pretty worthless if the data could not be accessed. Oracle supplies a number of views that can be queried that will provide direct access into the data dictionary tables. These views are generally tuned by Oracle for quick access to the underlying objects, and the names of the views often reflect the use of that view much better than the names of the underlying objects. The data dictionary views come in three main types:

- User views

- All views

- DBA views

To look at user information, there are three views, *user_users*, *all_users* and *dba_users*. Each of these views sees the user a bit differently.

All views that start with *user* only see the information that pertains to the user that is logged in. For example, if the user called SCOTT is logged in, when looking at the *user_tables* view, only information on tables that are owned by the SCOTT user can be seen. Although the user might have access to tables in the GEORGE schema, they cannot be seen in the *user_tables* view. Here is an example of a simple query against the *user_tables* view:

```
SELECT table_name FROM user_tables;
```

The *all* views allow a user to see all objects to which they have access. For example, if a user is logged in as SCOTT and queries the *all_tables* view, all the tables owned by SCOTT will be displayed and the user will also see any tables he has been granted access to that are owned by GEORGE, or any other user. The user has to have access rights to these objects, which he would have received via the GRANT command covered earlier.

Generally the two main differences between the *user* and *all* views are that the owner of the object is included in the *all* views, and not included in the *user* views. This makes sense since the user will only be seeing their objects. In this example, the *all_tables* view is queried for all tables that start with EMP:

```
SELECT
    table_name
FROM
    all_tables
```

```
WHERE
   table_name LIKE 'EMP%';
```

The granddaddies of the data dictionary views are the *dba* views. These views are unrestricted windows into all Oracle data dictionary objects. Because of this, they are only accessible by DBA's, as the name seems to suggest. All *dba* views start with *dba*. In this example, the *dba_tables* view is queried for all tables that start with EMP and are owned by users whose names start with RAMPANT:

```
SELECT
   table_name
FROM
   dba_tables
WHERE
   table_name LIKE 'EMP%'
AND
   owner like 'RAMPANT%';
```

The data dictionary tables are documented in the Oracle Database 10g Reference Guide, which is part of the overall Oracle database documentation set. There are almost 600 *dba* views in Oracle Database 10g alone, and a like number of *user* and *all* views. The *all* and *user* views are pretty much children of the *dba* views, and not every *all* or *user* view can be found for each *dba* view. The views are documented within the data dictionary itself. The *dictionary* or *dict* view contains all the tables of the data dictionary, plus comments for what each table is used.

Using the Data Dictionary

Like many things, using the data dictionary takes some practice. It takes understanding what needs to be found, figuring out how to find the view, and then looking at the view. Sometimes, of course, it may be necessary to join two, three, or more views together to find the answer.

This section will provide example queries against the data dictionary. These will be queries that many DBA's use when they are starting out. Most DBA's have a collection of data dictionary scripts right at hand.

Examples will be presented on how to:

- Determine what users are setup in the database

- Determine what tablespaces are configured in the database and where the related datafiles are located.

- Determine who owns a specific table and its tablespace.

- Determine what indexes are associated with a specific table.

The goal of presenting these examples is to provide some insight into how the data dictionary can be used to manage a database.

Learning by example

These examples are designed to provide ideas of how the data dictionary views can be used to manage a database. Very often, good DBA's will put scripts together that run on a regular schedule via CRON or some other scheduling facility. These scripts will monitor the database looking for problems, like running out of disk space.

There are tons of scripts out on the internet that can be used for this purpose. Since it is helpful to understand what the scripts are actually doing, these examples should provide some guidance. Use them to explore how the data dictionary works, and to see the powerful information it provides.

Determine What Users Exist in the Database

The following query will provide a list of current users in the database and it uses the *dba_users* data dictionary view. The default and temporary tablespace settings for these users are also included to insure those tablespaces are configured for a tablespace other than the SYSTEM tablespace. This is a common problem in databases that are not properly configured, especially Oracle 9i databases.

There are also some SQL*Plus formatting commands included so the output will be easy to read. That is one of the problems with the data dictionary, often the columns will run off the end of the screen. Use the SET LINES and COLUMN commands, as seen in the following example, to get output that is much easier to read.

```
SQL> set lines 80
SQL> column username format a20
SQL> column default_tablespace format a20
SQL> column temporary_tablespace format a20


SQL> Select username, default_tablespace, temporary_tablespace
2 From dba_users
3 Order by username;

USERNAME              DEFAULT_TABLESPACE    TEMPORARY_TABLESPACE
--------------------  --------------------  --------------------
MDDATA                USERS                 TEMP
MDSYS                 SYSAUX                TEMP
MGMT_VIEW             SYSAUX                TEMP
OLAPSYS               SYSAUX                TEMP
ORDPLUGINS            SYSAUX                TEMP
ORDSYS                SYSAUX                TEMP
OUTLN                 SYSTEM                TEMP
SCOTT                 USERS                 TEMP
```

Examine tablespaces and datafiles

This next query can be very helpful when the DBA is trying to understand what tablespaces are in a database and what datafiles are associated with those tablespaces. In this query, *dba_data_files* is used to extract each tablespace name, the datafile associated with that tablespace, and the size of the datafile. The query also joins *dba_free_space* to determine how much free space is left in the tablespace. This helps with planning future growth. Again,

SQL*Plus commands have been included to make the report easier to read.

```
SQL>BREAK ON tablespace_name SKIP 2
SQL>COMPUTE SUM OF allocated_bytes, free_bytes ON tablespace_name
SQL>COLUMN allocated_bytes FORMAT 9,999,999,999
SQL>COLUMN free_bytes FORMAT 9,999,999,999

SQL>SELECT a.tablespace_name, a.file_name, a.bytes allocated_bytes,
2 b.free_bytes
3 FROM dba_data_files a,
4 (SELECT file_id, SUM(bytes) free_bytes
5 FROM dba_free_space b GROUP BY file_id) b
6 WHERE a.file_id=b.file_id
7 ORDER BY a.tablespace_name;

TABLESPACE_NAME FILE_NAME                ALLOCATED_BYTES  FREE_BYTES
--------------- -----------------------  ---------------  -----------
TBS_LOCALS      /u01/app/oradata/devdb/de    20,971,520  20,774,912
                vdb/devdb_tbs_locals_01.d
                bf

* * * * * * * * * * * * * * *                 ---------------  -----------
sum                                          20,971,520  20,774,912


TBS_TOURISTS    /u01/app/oradata/devdb/de    20,971,520   8,257,536
                vdb/devdb_tbs_tourists_01
                .dbf

* * * * * * * * * * * * * * *                 ---------------  -----------
sum                                         199,229,440 176,291,840


USERS           /u01/app/oradata/devdb/de   112,721,920     655,360
                vdb/users01.dbf

* * * * * * * * * * * * * * *                 ---------------  -----------
sum                                         112,721,920     655,360
```

Queries like this make for great monitoring; although it would probably be useful to further restrict the rows that are returned to those where the tablespace has only five or ten percent free space available. The point is that there are a number of different ways of looking at this data and querying the data dictionary, but the DBA will have to dig into the data dictionary and learn it before being able to best utilize such queries.

⊞ Type the following string into the Google search engine to find more information: **bc oracle tablespace scripts**

Table and tablespace location

Finding out who owns a table and what tablespace it is in is a pretty common need of the DBA. In this query, the *dba_tables* view is used to find the owner and tablespace name of the EMP table.

```
SQL>  select owner, table_name, tablespace_name
  2    from dba_tables
  3    where table_name='EMP';

OWNER                TABLE_NAME           TABLESPACE_NAME
-------------------- -------------------- -------------
SCOTT                EMP                  USERS
POLL                 EMP                  USERS
```

As can be seen from this query, there are two tables called EMP, owned by two different users, Scott and Poll. Both tables are contained in the USERS tablespace.

A good exercise for an aspiring DBA might be to try to join this query with a view like *dba_extents* and figure out just how much space these tables are allocated. Give it a try, it is not hard!

See the indexes on a table

It is not unusual to wonder what indexes a specific table might have, and what columns in the table are assigned to those indexes. The following query will provide this information. It draws on the information in the *dba_ind_columns* data dictionary view:

```
SQL> column table_owner format a15
SQL> column table_name format a20
SQL> column index_name format a20
SQL> column column_name format a20

SQL> Select owner, table_name, index_name, column_name
```

```
2   FROM dba_ind_columns
3   Order by owner, table_name, column_position
4   Where owner='SCOTT'
5   AND table_name='EMP';

TABLE_OWNER      TABLE_NAME           INDEX_NAME
COLUMN_NAME
---------------  -------------------- -------------------- ----------
SCOTT            EMP                  PK_EMP               EMPNO
```

In this example, the EMP table in the SCOTT schema has one index called PK_EMP. This index is built on a single column, EMPNO.

The Dynamic Performance Views

This section explores the dynamic performance views. These views are very helpful in monitoring a database for real time performance. The following topics will be covered:

- The purpose of the Dynamic Performance Views

- The architecture of the Dynamic Performance Views

- Uses of the Dynamic Performance Views

⊡ Type the following string into the Google search engine to find more information: **bc oracle v$**.

The purpose of the Dynamic Performance Views

The dynamic performance views, often referred to as the *v$* views, are real-time or almost real time views into the guts of Oracle. What is the difference between the data dictionary views and the *v$* views? The data dictionary views can be thought of like a parts manual. It lists all the parts of the car and shows pictures of where they are located. This is quite handy if the DBA is trying to find where something is or if a part needs to be replaced, but not so helpful if all that needs to be done is the timing adjusted.

The $v\$$ views are like the speedometer and the tachometer in a car. They tell how fast the database is going or not going, and like the timing light in a car, they help adjust the database to improve performance. They provide almost immediate feedback as to the condition of the database.

The architecture of the Dynamic Performance Views

The basic foundation of the dynamic performance views is a set of very low level Oracle views that may rarely, if ever, need to be accessed. These views are called the $x\$$ views. The $x\$$ views are very low level representations of Oracle internal database structures. They are not tables, but database representation of C structures that are maintained by the Oracle kernel.

The naming conventions of the $x\$$ views and the columns in these views is so convoluted that even experienced DBA's do not want to have to go looking into them.

⌨ Type the following string into the Google search engine to find more information: **bc oracle x$**.

Oracle has created a very complete set of views called the $v\_\$$ views that overlay the $x\$$ views Oracle then provides synonyms that have the $v\$$ names that point to the $v\_\$$ views. In the end, when the DBA wants access to real time database information, it is the $v\$$ synonyms that will be used, although they are commonly referred to as $v\$$ views, go figure!

One last thing to note is that only those with DBA privileges have access to the $v\$$ views. There are ways around this, but it requires some rather advanced DBA work. That is beyond the scope of this book and the reader will just need to do some research on their own to find the answer.

Uses of the *v$* Views

As with the earlier section on the data dictionary views, it will be worthwhile to provide some examples of how the *v$* views are used. Again, the whole idea here is to contemplate how the *v$* views can be used to monitor databases performance. In the end, there are a ton of scripts out on the internet that can be used to perform just about any function a DBA needs. Here is a short list of some example uses of the *v$* views:

- See who is on the system

- See what SQL users are running on the system

- See what session is blocking other sessions

- See what waits are occurring in a database.

Viewing current Oracle users

One thing DBA's want to know is who is on the system. The following query is a good introduction to the *v$* views. It uses the *v$session* view to show who is currently connected to the database.

```
SQL> select sid, serial#, username, osuser, machine from v$session
  2 where username is not NULL;

SID    SERIAL# USERNAME                      OSUSER      MACHINE
---  ---------- -----------------------    ---------- -------------
122     49671 GRUMPY                        grummy      htmldb.com
141     45178 IMPORTANT_STUFF               oracle      htmldb.com
```

Notice in the results of this query the SID and SERIAL# columns. These columns individually identify each user session. The USERNAME columns shows the Oracle username of the person signed into the system, and the OSUSER column shows the OS username that the person used to sign into. These two columns can be very handy when trying to figure out who is actually connected to the system. For example, if the DBA is on a

UNIX system, he can run the finger command on the GRUMPY user, and possibly find out GRUMPY's identity:

```
SQL> host finger grumpy
Login: grumpy                        Name: Mike Dwarf Sr.
Directory: /home/grumpy              Shell: /bin/bash
On since Mon Sep  5 21:30 (EDT) on pts/4 from c-67-163-49-
102.hsd1.il.comcast.net
No mail.
No Plan.
```

The results show that Grumpy is actually Mike Dwarf Sr. If Mike is not supposed to be on the system, it may be time to make a phone call.

There are a number of these *v$* views in Oracle, providing a wealth of information. They are documented in the Oracle Database 10g Reference Guide.

See what SQL users are running on the system

Once the DBA figures out who is on the system, he will probably want to know what they are doing. In this case, the *v$session* view will be joined with the *v$sql* view. The *v$sql* view will provide the SQL that is being executed on the system. The following are GRUMPY's session details:

```
SQL> select a.sid, a.serial#, b.sql_text
  2  from v$session a, v$sqlarea b
  3  where a.sql_address=b.address
  4  and a.username='GRUMPY';

     SID    SERIAL# SQL_TEXT
---------- ---------- -----------------------------------------
     122      61521 select count(*) from gen_person where
gen_person_id=95000
```

See what session is blocking other sessions

Blocking sessions are a problem for the DBA and the DBA needs a way to find them so they can be dealt with. Blocking sessions occur when a session issues an insert, update or delete command that changes a row. When the change occurs, the row is locked until the session either commits the change, rolls the change back, or the user logs off the system. Problems might occur, for example, is a user makes a change and then forgets to commit the change before leaving for the weekend without logging off the system.

This query can be used to find these nasty blocking sessions. The *v$session* view is used to find the blocking session and also the sessions locked by that session.

```
SQL>  Select blocking_session, sid, serial#, wait_class,
  2   seconds_in_wait
  3   From v$session
  4   where blocking_session is not NULL
  5   order by blocking_session;

BLOCKING_SESSION        SID    SERIAL# WAIT_CLASS SECONDS_IN_WAIT
---------------- ---------- ---------- ---------- ---------------
             148        135      61521       Idle              64
```

In this case, session 148 is blocking session 135 and has been for 64 seconds. The next step would be to find out who is running session 148, and go find them and see why they are having a problem.

See what waits are occurring in the database.

In the final example demonstrating the power of the *v$* views, the DBA can see what waits are happening in a database. Waits are conditions where a session is waiting for something to happen. Waits can be caused by a number of things from slow disks, to locking situations, to various kinds of internal Oracle contention.

Waits come in two main kinds, system-level and session-level. The system-level waits represent a high level summary of all session-level waits. Session-level waits are session specific waits for specific sessions.

System waits come in different wait classes. Classes such as idle waits have no real impact on the database at all in most cases, although there are some rare exceptions. The current wait class waits can be viewed by querying the *v$system_wait_class* view as in the following example:

```
SQL> Select wait_class, sum(time_waited),
sum(time_waited)/sum(total_waits)
2 Sum_Waits
3 From v$system_wait_class
4 Group by wait_class
5 Order by 3 desc;


WAIT_CLASS       SUM(time_waited)  SUM_WAITS
---------------  ----------------  ----------
Idle                  9899040431  151.750403
Application              3147344  77.2183812
Concurrency              491226  26.0846432
Other                    431875  6.65036957
Administrative              718  5.52307692
Configuration           23691  1.85114862
Commit                  89282  .302570846
User I/O              2826520  .289489185
System I/O            646700   .1372763
Network              415446  .007569151
```

Note that in this output, the idle wait class far outweighs the other wait event classes, which is often the case for healthy databases. However, there are some other waits of interest; particularly it seems the application and concurrency waits have some time accumulated. The DBA will want to determine what waits are causing the problems.

This is done by drilling down to the next level of wait events using the *v$system_event* view. This gives more detailed wait event information, and the waits can be associated with the wait classes as can be seen in the following SQL:

```
SQL> Select a.event, a.total_waits, a.time_waited, a.average_wait
   2  From v$system_event a, v$event_name b, v$system_wait_class c
   3  Where a.event_id=b.event_id
   4  And b.wait_class#=c.wait_class#
   5  And c.wait_class in ('Application','Concurrency')
   6  order by average_wait desc;
```

```
EVENT                          TOTAL_WAITS time_waited average_wait
------------------------------ ----------- ----------- ------------
enq: TX - row lock contention       10669     3197011          300
buffer busy waits                   14218      470221           33
library cache pin                     270        4462           17
library cache load lock               177        1783           10
latch: library cache                 3673       14115            4
latch: cache buffers chains           329         494            2
latch: In memory undo latch            13          26            2
row cache lock                          2           4            2
latch: library cache lock              55          46            1
latch: library cache pin               95          74            1
enq: RO - fast object reuse           303          49            0
enq: TM - contention                    1           0            0
SQL*Net break/reset to client       29689        1106            0
SQL*Net break/reset to dblink         280           1            0
```

In this report, the top problem appears to be Enqueue waits. The enq: TX – row lock contention event is an enqueue. There are a huge number of events in Oracle Database 10g so it is not practical to know what each one means. They are all documented in the Oracle reference guide. Also, a search engine such as Google can be used to search for the event. Often there will be someone who had problems with it and there will be lots of help offered for correcting the problem.

In this case, an Enqueue wait has to do with the blocking locks presented earlier in this chapter. In Oracle, an enqueue is just another word for lock. If an experienced DBA saw that this was the big problem, they would start monitoring the sessions to try to figure out what is causing locking issues.   It is possible to drill down even further into the session level if needed. In this case, this query will determine if anyone is still causing locking:

```
SQL> select a.sid, a.event, a.total_waits, a.time_waited, a.average_wait
  2  from v$session_event a, v$session b
  3  where time_waited > 0
  4  and a.sid=b.sid
  5  and b.username is not NULL
  6 and a.event='enq: TX - row lock contention';

       SID EVENT                          TOTAL_WAITS time_waited average_wait
---------- ------------------------------ ----------- ----------- ------------
       110 enq: TX - row lock contention           14        4211          301
```

Note the TIME_WAITED and AVERAGE_WAIT columns are in Centaseconds in this view. To see the time in seconds, the time would have to be divided by 100. The system has waited for this blocking lock for four seconds so far. SID 110 is blocked right now!! The query presented earlier can be run to see who is blocking this session:

```
SQL> Select blocking_session, sid, serial#, wait_class,
  2  seconds_in_wait
  3  From v$session
  4  where blocking_session is not NULL
  5  order by blocking_session;

BLOCKING_SESSION        SID   SERIAL# WAIT_CLASS     SECONDS_IN_WAIT
---------------- ---------- ---------- ------------- ---------------
             161        110       561 Application                246
```

This is clearly a problem. The block continues to be held, now 246 seconds into the blocking event! The DBA needs to find out who SID 161 is and run them out of town. That is done with the query presented at the beginning of this section with a slight modification:

```
SQL> select sid, serial#, username, osuser, machine from v$session
  2 where username is not NULL;

       SID    SERIAL# USERNAME          OSUSER     MACHINE
---------- ---------- --------------- ---------- --------------------
       161      43123 GRUMPY            grummy     htmldb.com
```

Grumpy is at it again!

Conclusion

The data dictionary is very handy for finding internal details. The data dictionary is the primary tool of the DBA it is a good idea to start learning how to formulate dictionary queries. When looking for a DBA job, interviewers will ask about this in a technical interview. It is imperative to show familiarity and ease of use with the data dictionary. Also, the Oracle documentation and other

Rampant books provide many examples of using these views to manage a database effectively.

The main points of this chapter included:

- The data dictionary contains data-about-data or Metadata inside special tables.

- Data Dictionary tables are grouped into DBA, with total access, ALL, for anyone granted access, and USER, only that user's objects.

- Oracle has internal tables called *x$* fixed tables to hold performance information.

- Oracle maps the *x$* tables into views beginning with *v$*.

- The *v$* views can be used to see everything inside an instance.

- More than 600 data dictionary scripts can be purchased at www.oracle-script.com.

- Rampant offers a free data dictionary poster. Just Google: **bc free 10g poster**.

The next chapter will cover Oracle backup & recovery, a critical area of database management.

Oracle Backup and Recovery

Protecting Databases

One of the most, if not the most important, jobs of the Oracle DBA is to ensure that the databases in their care are protected. Databases, or data in the database, can be lost through a variety of ways including:

- User error

- Hardware failure

- Software failure

- Disasters

- Application errors

To protect their databases, DBA's will need to know how to back up and recover their databases. Backup and recovery is what this last chapter is all about. Backup and recovery can be a very difficult and complex topic. There are a number of different options to choose from when it comes to backing up a database. This Chapter is designed to set the aspiring DBA on the right course by describing how to perform basic database backup and recovery operations.

The Oracle RMAN tool will be used in this Chapter. It comes with the Oracle RDBMS and it is free. Topics that will be covered include:

- Backing up a database with RMAN

- Restoring a database with RMAN

So, without further delay, it is time to get started on the topic of backing up a database.

Backup a Database with RMAN

Database backups with RMAN are actually quite easy. The database can be in one of two modes, ARCHIVELOG or NOARCHIVELOG mode. The mode the database is in determines what kinds of backups can be performed on the database.

Starting RMAN

The RMAN client is started from the operating system prompt. To use RMAN, simply set the Oracle environment as it would be se before using any other Oracle client, such as SQL*Plus. Once the environment is set, then RMAN can be stated as shown in the following example:

```
rman target=/
```

Once RMAN is started, the RMAN prompt will be displayed. The system is ready to begin the database backup.

Perform an Offline (Cold) Backup of the Database with RMAN

This section will cover how to perform an offline, or cold, backup using RMAN. This will require that the database be down which is why it is called an offline backup. Oracle also supports online backups, and that will be covered shortly.

Before RMAN can be used, a few setting need to be configured. In this section, the database will be configured for the backup, and will then proceed to do the backup.

Configure the Database and RMAN for Backup

Before using RMAN, a few settings need to be configured. This section makes the following assumptions:

- /u01/app/oracle/backup is the name of the destination backup file. The DBA will need to create this file system if it does not already exist.

- That an SPFILE is being used.

Use of the SPFILE was described earlier in the book.

The configuration is pretty basic. First, a couple of database parameters need to be configured. These parameters will configure the Flash Recovery Area of the database. This is the location that all the disk backups will be made to. To configure the flash recovery area, the *alter system* command is used to set the value of two database parameters:

- **db_recovery_file_dest** – Determines the location of the flash recovery area.

- **db_recovery_file_dest_size** – Determines how much space can be used by Oracle in the flash recovery area.

The flash recovery area will be assigned a value of /u01/app/oracle/backup, and it will be assigned a 2 Gigabyte limit.

The following factors may play a role in the size of the flash recovery area:

- The size of the database

- The number of backups that need to be kept

- Whether or not the database if running in ARCHIVELOG mode, which will be covered in more detail later in the Chapter.

Here is an example of configuring the flash recovery as described previously. This assumes the database is using an SPFILE:

```
Alter system set db_recovery_file_dest='/u01/app/oracle/backup';
Alter system set db_recovery_file_dest_size=2G;
```

A couple of RMAN settings need to be configured before performing the first backup. First, start RMAN as detailed earlier in this section. Now, configure the following:

- Automatic backups of the control file and SPFILE.

- Retention policy to a redundancy of 2

The RMAN CONFIGURE command is used to adjust these settings as seen in the following example:

```
-- Configure the retention policy to redundancy of 2.
-- This means RMAN will try to keep 2 copies of the database
backups.

RMAN> configure retention policy to redundancy 2;

-- Configure automated backups of the control file and SPFILE.

RMAN>configure controlfile autobackup on;
```

Now that RMAN and the database are configured, the next step is to backup the database.

Performing the Offline Backup

Recall that an offline backup is a backup of the database while it is not running. Hence, to perform the backup the database will be shutdown from RMAN and then the database will be mounted. The backup will be performed. Once the backup is complete, the database will be restarted. Here is an example of this process:

```
RMAN>shutdown immediate
RMAN>startup mount
RMAN>backup database;
RMAN>sql 'alter database open';
```

Once this process is complete, the first backup has been accomplished. Recall that a redundancy of two was configured for the backups. RMAN will reclaim the space from the flash recovery area automatically as required, removing all unneeded backups. Later in this chapter, how to recover a database from this backup will be covered.

Performing Online Backups

As the name implies, an online backup allows the database to be backed up while users are working. Some newer DBA's are a little hesitant to perform online backups, thinking that somehow they might not work. Experienced DBA's will tell them that a correctly done online backup will be recoverable. Most shops these days use online backups at least for their production systems. For a large number of shops online backups are the only backups they ever make.

This section will walk through doing an online backup. First, the database needs to be put in ARCHIVELOG mode.

🖳 Type the following string into the Google search engine to find more information: **bc oracle rman backup**

The next steps are the configuration steps detailed in the previous section titled: *Configure the Database and RMAN for Backup*. Once that is done, it is time to proceed with the online backup with RMAN.

Perform an Online (Hot) Backup of the Database with RMAN

Once the database and RMAN have been setup to support hot backups, doing the backup is easy. In fact, it takes fewer RMAN commands than an offline backup does. Here is the RMAN command that should be used to kick off a database backup:

```
RMAN>backup database plus archivelogs delete input;
```

This command will backup the database. Along with the database backup, it will backup all the archived redo logs that have been generated by the database. Archived redo logs were covered in an earlier Chapter in the book. These archived redo logs are very important to the recovery of the database so they are backed up at the same time.

The archived redo logs can be backed up by themselves from time to time by issuing the following command:

```
RMAN>backup archivelogs all delete input;
```

Both of these examples use the DELETE INPUT command. This will cause the source archive redo logs to be removed once they are backed up. There is not need to worry since the DELETE INPUT command will not try to delete the database or datafiles. There are a number of other options that the aspiring DBA may want to explore with regards to backup retention and archived redo log retention. Check out Robert Freeman's other book, *Oracle9i RMAN Backup and Recovery* and *Oracle Database 10g RMAN Backup and Recovery* for more information on various aspects of RMAN.

Recovery of the Database with RMAN

When the chips are down, this is what it is all about for a DBA. Being able to recover a database is priority number one, compared to everything else. This section is about using the backups that were made earlier in this chapter to recover a database.

Recovery is one of the most complex Oracle topics. This section addresses basic recovery scenarios. More complicated recovery issues such as incomplete recovery or point in time recovery are covered in Robert Freeman's other titles, *Oracle9i RMAN Backup and Recovery* and *Oracle Database 10g RMAN Backup and Recovery*.

Recover a Database using an Offline Backup with RMAN

Before the database can be restored using RMAN, the following needs to be properly in place. This scenario this assumes a full system loss:

- The operating system must be installed
- The Oracle software must be installed
- The RMAN backup files must be available
- The file systems that the database files will be restored to must be created.

Once these pieces are in place the database can be restored. In the event of a full system loss the following will need to be replaced:

- The SPFILE
- The Control File
- The database datafiles

If the SPFILE or control file is intact, that component will not need to be replaced. The following sections walk through each restore step. This assumes that the backup procedures described earlier in this chapter were followed, which included the automated backup of SPFILE's and control files.

Restoring the SPFILE

Restoring the SPFILE is an automated process with RMAN in many cases. RMAN simply needs to be configured with the proper database DBID, which should have been recorded when the database was created. The SPFILE can then be restored from any auto backup.

To restore the SPFILE, the database will need to be started, and this can be done with a minimal database parameter file. To start the database instance, set the *db_name* parameter in a manual parameter file. Then the instance can be started using the STARTUP command with the *pfile* parameter as seen in the following example:

```
Startup nomount
pfile=c:\oracle\product\10.1.0.3\database\initbooktst.ora
```

Once the instance is started, RMAN can be started and used to restore the SPFILE as seen in the following example:

```
RMAN>restore spfile from autobackup;
```

If automated backups are not being used, it will be necessary to use more sophisticated means of restoring the SPFILE. This topic is beyond the scope of this book.

Restoring the Control File

Restoring the control file is much like restoring the SPFILE. Configure RMAN with the proper database DBID and then restore the control file from any auto backup.

To restore the CONTROL FILE, the database needs to be started, but again, it can be done with a minimal database parameter file. To start the database instance, the *db_name* parameter needs to be set in a manual parameter file. Then the instance can be started using the STARTUP command with the *pfile* parameter as seen in the following example:

```
Startup nomount
pfile=c:\oracle\product\10.1.0.3\database\initbooktst.ora
```

Once the instance is started, RMAN can be started and used to restore the CONTROL FILE as seen in the following example:

```
RMAN>restore control file from autobackup;
```

If automated backups are not being used, more sophisticated means of restoring the CONTROL FILE will have to be used, which are beyond the scope of this book.

Restoring and Recovering the Database

Once the SPFILE and the control file are restored, then restoring the database can be pretty easy. Again, many things can occur to make the process more complex, but assuming that the RMAN backup sets have been restored in the same place, and that all of the file systems are built correctly and named the same as before, the database can be restored with the following command:

```
RMAN>restore database noredo;
```

If the online archived redo logs are available, then change the command to the following:

```
RMAN>restore database;
```

Once the database is restored, then the database can be recovered. Simply use the RMAN RECOVER DATABASE command as seen in the following example:

```
RMAN>recover database;
```

Once this command has been issued, the database should be recovered to the point of the backup.

Recover a Database using an Online Backup with RMAN

If the ARCHIVELOG mode database was backed up with RMAN then it can be recovered to the point of the last available archived redo log or online redo log if those are still available. The cool thing is that the RMAN procedure is almost the same regardless of whether the backup was in ARCHIVELOG mode or NOARCHIVELOG mode.

First, follow the directions above for restores of the SPFILE and the CONTROL FILE. Now, simply use the RESTORE DATABASE and RECOVER DATABASE commands as seen in the following example:

```
RMAN>restore database;
RMAN>recover database;
```

This will cause the database to be restored. It will also automatically recover the archived redo logs.

Other RMAN Recovery Options

There are a number of other recovery options available with RMAN. Many of these can be complex. In fact, there is a 600 page book dedicated just to RMAN operations alone. Operations such as point in time recovery, incomplete recovery, and many others are possible with RMAN. RMAN is a very powerful backup and recovery tool and it is worth taking the time to learn.

Conclusion

Backing up a database is absolutely imperative. Without doing so, the DBA creates a major liability on their job as well as the company's existence. Experienced DBA's have seen databases crash without a good backup, and it is not pretty at all. It is something a DBA can easily lose their job over, and if it causes major problems, the DBA's credibility in the database world is at risk. The old line "you'll never work in this town again!" could have easily been said to a DBA who did not use RMAN to backup their database before it crashed, causing an entire company to cease to exist.

Remember, DBA's make their living off of their databases. A DBA's livelihood is at risk if their database has a chance of ever being lost without possible recovery.

Get creative with backups. Make sure to get everything, and then get it again. Never leave a file behind; one lost archivelog, one lost datafile, and the database will never be the same.

SQL and SQL*Plus

This is an excerpt from the bestselling book *Easy Oracle SQL* by John Garmany, published by Rampant TechPress.

Relational databases and SQL were developed in the early 1970's at IBM. SQL stands for Structured Query Language. The idea was to define a common method of storing data that would allow for the retrieval of specific information without detailed knowledge of the underlying database engine. In 1979, Oracle released the first commercial relational database that used SQL.

In 1986, the American National Standards Institute (ANSI) began publishing SQL standards. SQL is currently the standard query method of all major database management systems.

All about SQL

In Oracle, SQL is divided into two basic groups: data definition language (DDL) or data manipulation language (DML). DDL is used to define objects within the database just as creating tables or indexes. DML is used to insert, update, and delete data in the database. Finally, there is data retrieval, which is the SELECT statement.

The examples in this book are created using SQL*Plus. SQL*Plus is the command line interface to the Oracle Database. The first step is to start SQL*Plus and connect to the database. In Windows, open a terminal window. In Linux/Unix go to the command line and ensure that the database environment is set. To start SQL*Plus just enter "sqlplus".

If the program is not found, make sure the ORACLE_HOME is set in the path.

```
[oracle@appsvr oracle]$ sqlplus
SQL*Plus: Release 10.1.0.2.0 - Production on Thu Jan 20 20:23:44
2005
Copyright (c) 1982, 2004, Oracle.  All rights reserved.
Enter user-name:
```

The example database is called DEVDB. The following example shows how to start SQL*Plus and log on using one command.

```
[oracle@appsvr oracle]$ sqlplus pubs/pubs@devdb
SQL*Plus: Release 10.1.0.2.0 - Production on Thu Jan 20 20:28:11
2005
Copyright (c) 1982, 2004, Oracle.  All rights reserved.
Connected to:
Oracle Database 10g Enterprise Edition Release 10.1.0.2.0 -
Production
With the Partitioning, OLAP and Data Mining options
SQL>
```

The log on format is:

```
username/password@database_service_name.
```

The database service name is the name of the entry in the *tnsnames.ora* file located in ORACLE HOME/ network/admin/tnsnames.ora. A DBA may be needed to set up the *tnsnames.ora* file. If SQL*Plus is running on the computer on which Oracle is installed, then the installation program created a *tnsnames* entry that matches the database name. For this example, it is DEVDB.

🖧 Type the following string into the Google search engine to find more information: **bc oracle tnsnames**

For security reasons in order to prevent someone from seeing a password, it is not required that the password be typed into the

---

command line. Leave it out and SQL*Plus will ask for it and not echo the password to the screen.

```
[oracle@appsvr oracle]$ sqlplus pubs@devdb
SQL*Plus: Release 10.1.0.2.0 - Production on Thu Jan 20 20:29:54
2005
Copyright (c) 1982, 2004, Oracle.  All rights reserved.
Enter password:
Connected to:
Oracle Database 10g Enterprise Edition Release 10.1.0.2.0 -
Production
With the Partitioning, OLAP and Data Mining options
SQL>
```

Now that the connection is established, it is time to get to the SQL. Look at the AUTHOR table. The details of what makes up the AUTHOR table can be obtained by describing the table.

```
SQL> desc author

 Name                                      Null?    Type
 ----------------------------------------- -------- ------------
 AUTHOR_KEY                                          VARCHAR2(11)
 AUTHOR_LAST_NAME                                    VARCHAR2(40)
 AUTHOR_FIRST_NAME                                   VARCHAR2(20)
 AUTHOR_PHONE                                        VARCHAR2(12)
 AUTHOR_STREET                                       VARCHAR2(40)
 AUTHOR_CITY                                         VARCHAR2(20)
 AUTHOR_STATE                                        VARCHAR2(2)
 AUTHOR_ZIP                                          VARCHAR2(5)
 AUTHOR_CONTRACT_NBR                                 NUMBER(5)
```

This command lists the columns and their definitions.

SQL*Plus places each command into a buffer. The SQL*Plus buffer can be edited, but it is more efficient to create and run scripts. When a command is entered, SQL*Plus will continue to place it into the buffer until it encounters a semicolon. This tells SQL*Plus to execute the command. The previous command can be re-executed by entering a forward slash (/) or by entering RUN. To list the current buffer, enter "L". When a carriage return is submitted without a semicolon, SQL*Plus assumes commands are still being entered and will provide another line.

The Windows version of SQL*Plus also has a command history that can be cycled through using the Up/Down arrows.

As the queries become more complicated, the user will want to be able to edit their queries. The easiest way to do this is to use the host command. Enter host notepad <filename> at the SQL prompt to open a text file in notepad. Write/edit the query, save and close the file, then execute it with the @<filename> command. To re-edit the file, hit the up arrow to bring the host command back, enter and edit the query. In this way, the user can quickly go from editing to execution and back to editing.

The SELECT statement

The SELECT statement is used to retrieve data from the database. The format is:

```
select columns from tables;
```

The following example will retrieve a list of author last names from a sample database.

```
SQL> SELECT author_last_name FROM author;

AUTHOR_LAST_NAME
----------------------------------------
jones
hester
weaton
jeckle
withers
petty
clark
mee
shagger
smith

10 rows selected.
```

In SQL*Plus, statements sent to the database must end with a semicolon. SQL*Plus will continue to add lines to the buffer until it get a semicolon. The command below will give the same

results.   Notice that if ENTER is pressed and there is no
semicolon, SQL*Plus assumes that another line is being entered.

```
SQL> SELECT
  2    author_last_name
  3  FROM
  4    author;

AUTHOR_LAST_NAME
----------------------------------------
jones
hester
weaton
jeckle
withers
petty
clark
mee
shagger
smith

10 rows selected.
```

This is important because formatting commands will help avoid
errors.   As queries become more complicated, formatting
becomes more important. To retrieve more than one column
from a table, they are listed and separated by a comma. The
order that the columns are listed in the query will be the order
that they are returned.

```
SQL> SELECT
  2    author_last_name,
  3    author_first_name,
  4    author_city
  5  FROM
  6    author;

AUTHOR_LAST_NAME               AUTHOR_FIRST_NAME    AUTHOR_CITY
------------------------------ -------------------- -----------------
jones                          mark                 st. louis
hester                         alvis                st. louis
weaton                         erin                 st. louis

AUTHOR_LAST_NAME               AUTHOR_FIRST_NAME    AUTHOR_CITY
------------------------------ -------------------- -----------------
jeckle                         Pierre               north hollywood
withers                        lester               pie town
petty                          juan                 happyville
```

```
AUTHOR_LAST_NAME              AUTHOR_FIRST_NAME    AUTHOR_CITY
----------------------------  -------------------  -----------------
clark                         louis                rose garden
mee                           minnie               belaire
shagger                       dirk                 cross trax


AUTHOR_LAST_NAME              AUTHOR_FIRST_NAME    AUTHOR_CITY
----------------------------  -------------------  -----------------
smith                         diego                tweedle

10 rows selected.
```

Here are a few points about queries.

- SQL is not case sensitive. Key words are in caps, but that is not a requirement. Case is important with regard to actual data, but only for the data. In other words, if the query is looking for "John", then "JOHN" and "john" will not be returned.

- Formatting makes the query more readable to humans; it has no effect on the results or the performance. Tabs can be used to indent; however, some programs do not play well with tabs so it is best to just indent with spaces.

- Oracle stores database metadata, table names, index names, etc., in upper case. User data is stored as it is entered.

At this point, the SALES table will be used to do some work with numbers. First, describe the table.

```
SQL> desc sales

Name                                      Null?    Type
----------------------------------------  -------  ------------
STORE_KEY                                          VARCHAR2(4)
BOOK_KEY                                           VARCHAR2(6)
ORDER_NUMBER                                       VARCHAR2(20)
ORDER_DATE                                         DATE
QUANTITY                                           NUMBER(5)
```

Now, retrieve a list containing the values in the columns called ORDER_NUMBERS and QUANTITY.

```
SQL> SELECT
  2      order_number,
  3      quantity
```

```
FROM
  sales;

ORDER_NUMBER              QUANTITY
-------------------- ----------
O101                       1000
O102                         10
O103                        200
O104                        400
O105                        800
O106                        180
O107                        900
.....
O198                       8900
O199                       8800

ORDER_NUMBER              QUANTITY
-------------------- ----------
O200                        100

100 rows selected.
```

For display purposes, the middle part has been removed from the result set. Notice that the character column is left justified and the number column is right justified. This is how SQL*Plus returns the data. The column heading can be changed by aliasing the columns. To alias a column, use the AS keyword. If the new column name includes a space, the alias needs to be enclosed in quotes.

```
SQL> SELECT
  2    order_number AS "Order Number",
  3    quantity qty
  4  FROM
  5    sales;

Order Number                  QTY
-------------------- ----------
O101                       1000
O102                         10
O103                        200
O104                        400
O105                        800
O106                        180
  . . .
```

To select all the columns in the sales table use the command "select * from sales".

```
SQL> SELECT * FROM sales;

STOR BOOK_K ORDER_NUMBER          ORDER_DAT   QUANTITY
---- ------ --------------------  --------- ----------
S101 B101   O101                  02-JAN-02       1000
S102 B102   O102                  02-JAN-02         10
S103 B102   O103                  02-JAN-02        200
S104 B102   O104                  03-JAN-02        400
S105 B102   O105                  03-JAN-02        800
S106 B103   O106                  03-JAN-02        180
S107 B103   O107                  04-JAN-02        900
 .   .   .
```

Math operations can also be performed on number columns. Math in SQL follows the normal order of precedence. Multiplication (*) and Division (/) operations are computed before Addition (+) and Subtraction (-). Operators of the same priority are evaluated left to right. Parentheses can be used to change the order of evaluation.

```
SQL> SELECT
  2     order_number Ord,
  3     quantity,
  4     2*quantity+10 num
  5  FROM
  6     sales;

ORD                      QUANTITY        NUM
-------------------- ---------- ----------
O101                       1000       2010
O102                         10         30
O103                        200        410
 .   .   .
```

Notice in the example above that the multiplication happened before the addition. A NULL value is a column value that has not been assigned or has been set to NULL. It is not a blank space or a zero. It is undefined. Because a NULL is undefined, there is no such thing as NULL math. A NULL + 4 = NULL. NULL * 3 = NULL. Since NULL is undefined, all mathematical operations using a NULL return a NULL.

Conclusion

The SELECT statement is the foundation of Oracle SQL, but there are many complex features of SQL that allow complex queries to be solved using Oracle SQL syntax. This is just a taste of Oracle SQL and *Easy Oracle SQL* is highly recommended for more complete details on using Oracle SQL to query a database.

The final chapter will provide a quick overview of the Oracle PL/SQL programming language to show how complex processing logic can be written and stored inside the Oracle database.

Programming in PL/SQL

This is an excerpt from the bestselling book *Easy Oracle PL/SQL Programming* by John Garmany, published by Rampant TechPress.

Introduction to PL/SQL

Databases have been in use long before the personal computer arrived on the scene. IBM developed the Structured Query Language standard (dubbed SQL, and pronounced "See-Quel") over 30 years ago as a way to retrieve data from their new relational database. A decade later, Oracle released the first commercial relational database that used SQL, and SQL has become the de-facto query language for the vast majority of popular database products.

Even though SQL is the standard language for interacting with most modern databases, it does not mean SQL is without limitations. Retrieving a set of records from the database and modify them according to a set of rules cannot be done with a single SQL call to the database. Complex processing requires the ability to compare values, often called Boolean logic, and implement programmatic flow control. In other words, some type of programming language was required to process the returned rows and implement the program rules. To achieve this capability, Oracle introduced the Procedural Language extensions to the Structured Query Language or PL/SQL.

Oracle PL/SQL was based on the ADA programming language which was developed by the Department of Defense to be used on mission critical systems. Although not a sexy language like Java or C, ADA is still being developed and used for applications such as aircraft control systems. ADA is a highly structured, strongly typed programming language that uses natural language constructs to make it easy to understand. The PL/SQL language inherited these attributes making PL/SQL easier to read and maintain than more cryptic languages such as C. For example, below are two loops, one in PL/SQL and the other in a programming language called C.

```
for x in v_start..v_finish --PL/SQL
loop
   v_int := v_int +1;
end loop;
```

As opposed to:

```
for (x = str; x< fin; x++) {i++}   --C
```

Although the PL/SQL statement is more verbose, it is easier to understand.

PL/SQL is also portable within the Oracle database family and runs on all supported Oracle platforms including Oracle10g grid database. Even more important is platform independence, where programs developed in PL/SQL on a Windows Oracle database will load and run in a UNIX Oracle database. With each release of the Oracle database, Oracle Corporation enhances the capabilities and performance of PL/SQL. Remember, PL/SQL is an Oracle only product, and no other database management system will run PL/SQL.

Unlike other languages that execute externally, PL/SQL executes inside the database. This means that the DBA can take advantage of PL/SQL's exceptional ability to manipulate data in the database without paying the network penalty of retrieving the data out of the database and them updating it back to the database. Because PL/SQL runs inside the database it takes advantage of the capabilities and capacity of the database server.

Traditionally, PL/SQL has been a compiled/interpreted language similar to Java. When PL/SQL code is loaded into the database it is compiled into an intermediate form, similar to the way Java is compiled into byte-code. This intermediate code is portable across Oracle databases. Later versions of Oracle, Oracle9i and 10g, will compile PL/SQL into native code for over 60 hardware platforms. This natively compiled code runs more efficiently, but it loses the ability to move to other Oracle databases without recompiling.

Lastly, placing the code that interacts with the database in PL/SQL makes better use of the database resources. PL/SQL packages are loaded as a package so as the program calls for data, the procedures and functions are already in cached memory. Using PL/SQL will also result in the application using bind variables. The only way not to use bind variables in PL/SQL is to implement dynamic SQL. The Database Administrator (DBA) also benefits when developers place their SQL inside PL/SQL because they have access to the statements for tuning. For example the DBA can tune the SQL by adding hints, reordering the WHERE clauses, etc., without impacting the existing application. Placing SQL inside PL/SQL also allows the code to be protected by the recovery capabilities of the Oracle database.

PL/SQL is the most common language for Oracle, and developers are realizing the benefits in both application performance and database performance by implementing the database interaction in PL/SQL. There are even websites built entirely using PL/SQL. For example, Oracle's HTML-DB product is installed in the database and consists primarily of PL/SQL packages and Java scripts.

PL/SQL Basic Structure

Like the ADA programming language, PL/SQL is based on blocks, and PL/SQL provides a number of different blocks for different uses. The characteristics of a block include:

- A block begins with a declarative section where variables are defined.

- This is followed by a section containing the procedural statements surrounded by the BEGIN and END keywords. Each block must have a BEGIN and END statement, and may optionally include an exception section to handle errors.

Here is an example of a simple block:

```
SQL> declare
  2    v_line varchar2 (40);
  3  begin
  4    v_line := 'Hello World';
  5    dbms_output.put_line (v_line);
  6  end;
  7  /

Hello World
```

In the example above, the variable *v_line* is defined in the declarative section on line 2. Like SQL statements, each line ends with a semicolon. Once *v_line* is defined, it can be used in the procedural section. First, *v_line* is assigned the literal string 'Hello World' on line 4. Strings are surrounded by single quotes in SQL and PL/SQL. The *v_line* variable is then placed in the output buffer using the procedure *dbms_output.put_line*.

In PL/SQL, the semicolon defines the end of a line of code. To execute the PL/SQL block, use the forward slash ("/") on a line by itself as shown on line 7. If the forward slash is forgotten, SQL*Plus will simply wait for the next line to be entered.

> **Note:** If a PL/SQL script is executed and SQL*Plus returns a number, this is probably an indication that the"/" was forgotten at the end of the script. SQL*Plus is actually waiting for the next line. Entering a "/" will execute the script.

A PL/SQL block with no name is called an anonymous block. It starts with the DECLARE keyword to define the declarative section.

```
declare
    …    define variables here
begin
    …    code goes here
exceptions
end;
```

A named block is a procedure or a function. The name portion defines the declarative section so the DECLARE keyword is not used.

```
create procedure my_proc
as
    …    define variables here
begin
    …    code goes here
exceptions
end;
```

A procedure can be passed and change variables. A function can be passed variables and must return a variable.

```
create function my_func (v_name varchar2) return number
as
    …    define variables here
begin
    …    code goes here
    return n_jobNum;
end;
```

When variables are passed to a procedure or function they can be IN, OUT or INOUT. An IN variable is passed into the procedure or function and is used, but can not be changed. An

OUT variable is passed to the procedure but it can be changed and left in the changed state when the procedure ends.

An INOUT variable is passed to a procedure or function, and it can be used by the block, changed by the block, and left in a changed state when the block ends. A function can only be passed an IN variable and must return a variable. This can be confusing.

Displaying PL/SQL Output

Another change with PL/SQL from SQL is that the database does not return the output. PL/SQL code normally will change data, insert values, and so forth, inside the database. It will not normally display results back to the user. To do this a procedure called *dbms_output.put_line* is used to place the results in a buffer that SQL*Plus will retrieve and display. SQL*Plus must be told to retrieve data from this buffer in order to display the results. The SQL*Plus command *set serveroutput on* causes SQL*Plus to retrieve and display the buffer.

```
SQL> declare
  2    v_line varchar2 (40);
  3  begin
  4    v_line := 'Hello World';
  5    dbms_output.put_line (v_line);
  6  end;
  7  /

PL/SQL procedure successfully completed.

SQL> set serveroutput on
SQL> declare
  2    v_line varchar2 (40);
  3  begin
  4    v_line := 'Hello World';
  5    dbms_output.put_line (v_line);
  6  end;
  7  /
Hello World

PL/SQL procedure successfully completed.
```

The first time the script is run, the result was just a notice that the script completed successfully. Once *set serverouput on* was set the script was rerun, the results are shown.

This is an anonymous block of PL/SQL code. It is sent to the database, compiled and executed, then SQL*Plus retrieves the results. The script is stored in the SQL*Plus buffer and can be rerun by executing the forward slash.

```
SQL> /
Hello World

PL/SQL procedure successfully completed.
```

The script is not stored in the database like a stored or named procedure. It must be resent to the database and compiled each time it is executed.

As with SQL statements, SQL*Plus variables can be used to make the PL/SQL script dynamic. Just as with a SQL statement, the variables are local to SQL*Plus and are substituted before the code is sent to the database.

```
SQL> declare
  2    v_line varchar2 (40);
  3  begin
  4    v_line := 'Hello &name';
  5    dbms_output.put_line (v_line);
  6  end;
  7  /
Enter value for name: John
old   4:   v_line := 'Hello &name';
new   4:   v_line := 'Hello John';
Hello John

PL/SQL procedure successfully completed
```

The SQL*Plus ACCEPT command is a more flexible method of embedding dynamic data in the script.

```
SQL> accept v_string prompt "Enter Your First Name: "

Enter Your First Name: Thomas
```

```
SQL> declare
  2    v_line varchar2 (40):= '&v_string';
  3  begin
  4    v_line := 'Hello '||v_line;
  5    dbms_output.put_line (v_line);
  6  end;
  7  /

old   2:   v_line varchar2 (40):= '&v_string';
new   2:   v_line varchar2 (40):= 'Thomas';

Hello Thomas

PL/SQL procedure successfully completed.
```

The following is a closer examination of this script. The first line is the SQL*Plus ACCEPT command to get the SQL*Plus variable *v_string*. This line must be executed alone, not part of the PL/SQL block. At the prompt, the name Thomas was entered. Now the script is run but it is slightly modified from previous examples.

```
SQL> declare
  2    v_line varchar2 (40):= '&v_string';
```

The variable *v_line* is declared as a *varchar2*(40) and is given a default value that equals *v_string*. The PL/SQL assignment operator (:=) is used to assign the value. Hence, *v_line* is a bucket that gets assigned the string 'Thomas'. A developer would read an assignment statement in English as "v_line gets v_string" to indicate the assignment. The following is a more complex assignment statement.

```
4    v_line := 'Hello '||v_line;
```

Line 4 uses the concatenate operator to append "Hello" to the front of *v_line* and then assigns it back to the variable *v_line*. The variable *v_line* now contains the string 'Hello Thomas'. Line 5 places the value of *v_line* in the buffer to be retrieved by SQL*Plus.

```
old   2:   v_line varchar2 (40):= '&v_string';
new   2:   v_line varchar2 (40):= 'Thomas';
```

These two lines demonstrate SQL*Plus's verify function showing what is substituted before the code is sent to the database for execution. This information can be switched on/off with the verify command

```
SQL> set verify on
SQL> set verify off
```

Variable Declaration and Conversion

In the previous examples a variable, *v_line,* was defined. All variables are defined in the declaration section of the block. Variables are defined in the form:

```
variableName      datatype      := defaultvalue;
```

Below are examples of variables. Variables can be defined as any valid datatype to include user defined datatypes and records.

```
declare
  v_str1    varchar2 (80);
  v_str2    varchar2 (30) := 'Hello World';
  d_today   date;
  n_sales   number;
  n_order   number(8);
begin
```

A constant is defined the same way a variable is with the key word CONSTANT.

```
c_standard constant number := 90;
```

Notice that a constant must be assigned a value. The statement shown above does four things:

- Names the variable *c_standard*

- Defines *c_standard* as a constant

Introduction to PL/SQL   **203**

- Defines *c_standard* as a numeric datatype

- Assigns a value of 90 to *c_standard*

With PL/SQL constants, note that a constant value cannot be changed unless it is redefined in a subsequent block.

In the examples above the two variables are defined as numbers. It is time to see how to include the precision and scale for a number. As in SQL, PL/SQL supports mathematical operations and has a large library of mathematical functions, covering everything from advanced multivariate statistics to Newtonian Calculus. PL/SQL also supports single-row functions to convert numbers to characters and characters to numbers.

IF/THEN/ELSE Statements

The IF/THEN statement checks a Boolean value or expression and if true, executes the statements in the THEN clause. If the condition is false, the statements in the THEN clause are skipped and execution jumps to the END IF. The expression that is checked must return a true or false. It can be a simple Boolean variable or a compound expression joined with AND/OR clauses. The expression can even be a PL/SQL function that returns a Boolean value.

There is no requirement to surround the expression with parenthesis but most developers use parentheses for clarity. The THEN clause can contain a single or multiple statements, or a nested PL/SQL block. Here is an example of a basic IF/THEN statement with a THEN clause.

```
if v_numb > 5 then
  v_numb  := 5;
  v_other := 10;
end if;
```

In the statements above, the Boolean condition *v_numb* > 5 must be true before the THEN clause is executed. If *v_numb* is equal to or less than 5, or if it evaluates to NULL, the program control jumps to the statement after the END IF clause. Note that the THEN clause can contain any number of valid PL/SQL statements. The variable *v_other* and *v_numb* will not change unless the condition is true.

Note: All the IF/THEN statements must end with an END IF clause. The PL/SQL engine will continue to include statements in the THEN clause until it encounters an END IF. If a compile error is encountered that states: "found xxxx when expecting IF", the compiler encountered an END statement before it encountered the END IF. Simply find the end of the IF statement and close it with an END IF to correct the problem.

Sometimes the program flow will want to branch one direction if the condition is true and another direction if the condition is false. This is handled within the IF/THEN/ELSE statement.

Like the IF/THEN statement, the THEN clause statements will only be executed if the condition is true. However if the condition is false, the statements in the ELSE clause are executed. This is an either-or situation.

```
if n_numb > 5 then
  v_status := 'large';
else
  v _status := 'small';
end if;
```

After executing the example, the variable *v_status* will be defined as either large or small. Note that the above statement could also be written as two separate IF statements.

```
if n_numb > 5 then v_status := 'large'; end if;
if n_numb <=5 then v_status := 'small'; end if;
```

Programmatically, the results are the same, however the two IF statements required two evaluations, while the IF/THEN/ELSE statement requires only one evaluation.

The PL/SQL WHILE Loop

The WHILE loop, which is also called a conditional loop, evaluates a condition before each loop executes. If the result is false, the loop is terminated. If the expression is false when the program reaches the WHILE loop, the loop code is jumped and never executed. Use a WHILE loop when the condition test is required at the start of the loop. The next example contains three WHILE loops.

```
SQL> declare
  2    v_test varchar2 (8) := 'RUN';
  3    n_numb number := 2;
  4  begin
  5    while v_test <> 'STOP' loop
  6      if n_numb > 5
  7        then v_test := 'STOP';
  8        end if;
  9      dbms_output.put_line (v_test||': '||n_numb);
 10      n_numb := n_numb + 1;
 11    end loop;
 12
 13    v_test := 'DOWN';
 14    while n_numb > 1 AND v_test = 'DOWN' loop
 15      dbms_output.put_line (v_test||': '||n_numb);
 16      n_numb := n_numb - 1;
 17    end loop;
 18
 19    while 7 = 4 loop
 20      NULL;  -- never get here
 21    end loop;
 22  end;
 23  /
RUN: 2
RUN: 3
RUN: 4
RUN: 5
STOP: 6
```

```
DOWN:  7
DOWN:  6
DOWN:  5
DOWN:  4
DOWN:  3
DOWN:  2
```

The last loop will never execute because the condition will never be true. The middle loop uses multiple condition tests, using the AND key word. The first loop runs while *v_test* does not equal 'STOP'. Notice that the check that changes *v_test* in lines 6, 7, 8 is at the top of the loop. This is a poor choice because even though *v_test* may change, it is not evaluated again until the program gets back to the top of the loop. This results in the output stopping after *n_numb* reached 6, but notice in the results that at completion of the first loop, *n_numb* was left with a value of 7. Unless this was the programmer's intent, a small, hard to locate bug has been introduced into the code.

The programmer must ensure that the order of the statements inside the loop will leave the variables in the required state when the loop terminates. Remember that the WHILE loop tests at the start of the loop and does not test again until the loop has completely run and returned to the loop start. Both the endless loop and the WHILE loop execute until a condition is met. These loops are effective if the programmer does not know how many times the loop will execute. If the loop will run for a specified number of iterations, it is more efficient to use a FOR loop.

The PL/SQL REPEAT-UNTIL Loop

The WHILE loop tests at the start of the loop and if the condition is false, the loop code is never executed. To ensure that the loop code is executed at least one, the test must be preformed at the bottom of the loop. This is referred to as a REPEAT-UNTIL or DO-WHILE loop. PL/SQL does not directly implement a REPEAT-UNTIL loop however it is easy to construct one using an endless loop. By placing the EXIT WHEN (condition = true) statement as the last line of code in an endless loop the same results can be achieved.

```
SQL> declare
  2    n_num number := 1;
  3  begin
  4    loop
  5      dbms_output.put(n_num||', ');
  6      n_num := n_num + 1;
  7      exit when n_num > 5;
  8    end loop;
  9    dbms_output.put_line('Final: '||n_num);
 10  end;
 11  /
1, 2, 3, 4, 5, Final: 6

PL/SQL procedure successfully completed.
```

Since the condition test is at the bottom of the loop, this ensures the loop code is executed at least once.

The PL/SQL FOR Loop

The FOR loop executes for a specified number of times as defined in the loop definition. Because the number of loops is specified, the overhead of checking a condition to exit is eliminated. The number of executions is defined in the loop definition as a range from a start value to an end value (inclusive). The integer index in the FOR loop starts at the start value and increments by one (1) for each loop until it reaches the end value.

```
SQL> begin
  2    for idx in 2..5 loop
  3      dbms_output.put_line (idx);
  4    end loop;
  5  end;
  6  /
2
3
4
5

PL/SQL procedure successfully completed.
```

In the example below a variable *idx* is defined and assigned the value of 100. When the FOR loop executes, the variable *idx* is also defined as the index for the FOR loop. The original variable *idx* goes out of scope when the FOR loop defines its index variable. Inside the FOR loop, the *idx* variable is the loop index. Once the FOR loop terminates, the loop index goes out of scope and the original *idx* variable is again in scope.

```
SQL> declare
  2    idx number := 100;
  3  begin
  4    dbms_output.put_line (idx);
  5    for idx in 2..5 loop
  6      dbms_output.put_line (idx);
  7    end loop;
  8    dbms_output.put_line (idx);
  9  end;
 10  /
100
2
3
4
5
100

PL/SQL procedure successfully completed.
```

The loop index can be used inside the loop, but its value cannot be changed. Looping by an increment other than one will have to be done programmatically because the FOR loop will only increment the index by one.

```
SQL> begin
  2    for i in 4 .. 200 loop
  3      i := i + 4;
  4    end loop;
  5  end;
  6  /
    i := i + 4;
    *
ERROR at line 3:
ORA-06550: line 3, column 5:
PLS-00363: expression 'I' cannot be used as an assignment target
ORA-06550: line 3, column 5:
PL/SQL: Statement ignored
```

The loop index start and stop values can be expressions or variables. They are evaluated once at the start of the loop to determine the number of loop iterations. If their values change during the loop processing, it does not impact the number of iterations.

```
SQL> declare
  2    n_start number := 3;
  3    n_stop  number := 6;
  4  begin
  5    for xyz in n_start .. n_stop loop
  6      n_stop := 100;
  7      dbms_output.put_line (xyz);
  8    end loop;
  9  end;
 10  /
3
4
5
6
```

Conclusion

This chapter is just a quick introduction to the powerful features of PL/SQL. PL/SQL is a complete language and it has many sophisticated operators to maximize the retrieval and storing of data.

For the complete story, the book *Easy Oracle PL/SQL Programming* is highly recommended. Once basic SQL has been mastered, a more advanced book may be used, *Oracle PL/SQL Tuning* by Dr. Timothy Hall.

Index

A

ACCEPT 201, 202
ADA...195, 198
ADDM.......................................12, 40
ALL PRIVILEGES option 151
all_ind_columns 134
all_indexes 134
all_tab_columns 114, 115
all_tables......................... 114, 115, 160
all_users 160
ALTER INDEX.......................... 129
ALTER TABLESPACE.....102, 103
ALTER TEMPORARY
    TABLESPACE...................... 102
American National Standards
    Institute...................................... 186
ANALYZE TABLE.................... 116
ANSI... 186
ANY keyword............................. 150
Application identifier.....................52
ARCH 92, 94
ARCHIVELOG mode 55, 91, 92,
    93, 94, 95, 178, 179, 184
Archiver Process 25
artificial intelligence 8, 11
auto... 121
Automated Workload Repository40,
    220
Automatic Database Diagnostic
    Monitor..40
autorun...42
AWR 40, 220

B

B*Tree indexes 125, 126, 128
background processes 10, 13, 21, 25,
    73, 81

background_dump_dest.......................81
backup 54, 55, 68, 83, 84, 91, 101,
    149, 175, 176, 184
Backup and recovery................... 175
bitmap join indexes 114
bitmapped index merge 132
Blocking sessions........................169
Boolean 204, 205
Boolean logic................................195
branch node..................................127
buffer cache....15, 16, 18, 22, 23, 32,
    57, 82

C

cascade...118
CASCADE 118
CHAR...106
CHECK CONSTRAINT 139
checkpoint process 23
COMMIT 19, 97
concatenated primary key............109
constant...203
CONSTANT...................................203
constraint ... 108, 109, 110, 113, 139,
    140, 141, 143
CONSTRAINT..............................139
CONTROL FILE 182, 183, 184
Control Structures 18
control_file 85
CREATE INDEX 128, 149
CREATE PUBLIC SYNONYM
   154
CREATE ROLE 156
CREATE SESSION....................149
CREATE SYNONYM 154
CREATE TABLE......106, 107, 108,
    109, 110, 134, 139, 142, 149
CREATE TABLESPACE............99

CREATE TEMPORARY
    TABLESPACE...................... 102
CREATE USER 145, 146
create users................... 105, 147, 148
CRON... 162

D

data definition language 186
data dictionary 18, 79, 80, 90, 96, 99,
    103, 114, 122, 129, 134, 136,
    158, 159, 161, 162, 163, 164,
    165, 166
data manipulation language 186
database block size.........................32
Database Buffer Cache 16
database storage parameters..........58
Database Writer...............................22
datafiles..... 22, 23, 27, 30, 32, 59, 73,
    74, 77, 78, 99, 100, 102, 103,
    162, 163, 180, 181
datatype...................................203, 204
DATE.. 106
db_block_size 16, 81
db_cache_size.........................15, 17, 57
db_file_multiblock_read_count 133
db_name.. 182
db_recovery_file_dest 82, 93, 177
db_recovery_file_dest_size.... 82, 83, 177
dba_all_tables.....................................79
dba_data_files...........................103, 163
dba_extents 165
dba_free_space............................ 163
dba_ind_columns.................134, 165
dba_ind_partitions 79
dba_ind_subpartitions...........................79
dba_indexes 79, 134
dba_object_tables...............................79
dba_part_col_statistics 79
dba_subpart_col_statistics 79
dba_tab_col_statistics.........................80
dba_tab_cols 79

dba_tab_columns 80, 114, 115
dba_tab_modifications 120
dba_tab_partitions..............................80
dba_tab_subpartitions 80
dba_tables.........79, 114, 121, 161, 165
dba_tablespaces.....................................103
dba_temp_files...............................103
dba_users 160, 162
DBCA..............48, 50, 54, 60, 61, 62
dbms_aqadm 38
dbms_output.put_line.............. 198, 200
dbms_repcat 38
dbms_scheduler....................124
dbms_stats 116, 117
dbms_utility....................................116
DDL 186
DECLARE...................................199
DEFAULT TABLESPACE.......146
DELETE INPUT 180
DESC 109
dict 161
DICT 80
dictionary cache 17, 18
disable...124
DML..186
DO-WHILE loop 207
DROP SYNONYM....................155
DROP TABLE............................113
DROP TEMPORARY
    TABLESPACE......................102
DROP USER 145, 148
Dynamic Performance Views.....166
dynamic SQL..................................197

E

ELSE clause 205
enable..124
END IF................................ 204, 205
Enqueue 172
Enterprise Edition.........................37
estimate_percent...........................120

EXIT WHEN............................ 208

F

flash recovery. 54, 55, 93, 94, 95, 96,
   177, 178, 179
FLASHBACK TABLE.......113, 114
FOR loop 207, 208, 209
FOREIGN KEY 139, 141, 142, 143
FULL SCAN............................... 116
function 199, 203

G

gather auto..................................... 120
gather empty 120
gather stale.................................... 120
gather_database_stats..........122, 123
gather_fixed 123
gather_schema_stats.. 117, 118, 122,
   123
gather_system_stats 119
gather_table_stats.....................117, 118
Google 172
GRANT....... 148, 149, 150, 151, 160

H

hash_area_size......................................20
HTML-DB.................................. 197

I

IBM 195
IDENTIFIED BY clause........... 146
idle wait class 171
IF/THEN 204, 205
IF/THEN/ELSE 204, 206
init.ora 28, 73, 80, 82, 86
initSID.ora 83, 84, 86
in-line constraint 108
IP 44
iSQL*Plus.......................................47

J

Java.. 196, 197
JDBC 62
Job Queue Process 24, 25
job scheduler 24, 25
job_queue_processes...........................25

L

LGWR...22
library cache................................... 17
Linux.................................8, 48, 84, 186
listener.ora.......................................29
Log Writer Process......................... 22
log_buffer......................................15, 18

M

Massively Parallel Processors........ 39
Metadata........................114, 158, 191
method_opt.................................121
MMAN.. 25
MMNL.. 25
MMON 25
multivariate statistics 204

N

Newtonian Calculus 204
NOARCHIVELOG mode. 91, 176,
   184
nomount............................. 72, 73, 74
NOT NULL.................110, 111, 140
NULL.......... 110, 140, 141, 193, 205

O

object privileges 148, 152
objects 30, 31, 32, 67, 101, 105, 113,
   118, 122, 135, 145, 148, 149,
   150, 151, 152, 154, 155, 156,
   157, 159, 160, 161, 186

OCI 62
ODBC..62
OEM 52, 62
OLAP...40
one-to-many relationship........... 142
Online Analytical Processing 40
Online Backup............................ 179
online redo logs 19, 22, 27, 28, 59,
    60, 88, 89, 90, 92, 93
optimizer 115, 116, 119
optional products 41
ORA-01555.....................................98
Oracle Corporation..................... 196
Oracle Enterprise Manager ... 40, 52,
    62
oracle_sid......................................72
Oracle10g 196
Oracle9i 197
out-of-line constraints 109

P

parameter file 28, 73, 80, 81, 182
partitioning.............................111, 128
Personal Edition.............................37
pfile..............................84, 85, 86, 182
PFILE 28, 81, 82, 83, 84, 86, 87
pga_aggregate_target 20
PL/SQL....................... 195, 198, 204
PL/SQL Area 18
PL/SQL packages........................ 197
PMON......................................23
predicate 137, 138
Predicate pushing.................137, 138
primary key. 108, 109, 110, 140, 141,
    142
PRIMARY KEY 108
primary key constraint 108, 113, 126
Private SQL Area 18
private synonym 154, 155
privileges...64, 66, 75, 148, 149, 150,
    151, 152, 153, 156, 167

procedure 198, 199, 200, 201
Program Global Area...............14, 19

Q

Queue Monitor Process................ 25
QUOTA keyword 146
QUOTA UNLIMITED keyword
   146

R

RAC 54
RAM memory 10, 13
range scans.................................. 126
RECOVER DATABASE.. 183, 184
redo log 15, 19, 22, 28, 30, 87, 88,
    89, 90, 92, 95, 96, 180, 184
redo log buffer 18, 19, 22
redo log group....... 28, 87, 88, 89, 90
REFERENCES keyword............ 143
release level 37
RENAME TO 102, 129
repeat.. 121
REPEAT-UNTIL loop 207
RESTORE DATABASE............184
restricted mode 75
revoke 150
REVOKE 149, 150, 151, 152
RMAN.... 83, 84, 175, 176, 177, 178,
    179, 181, 182, 183, 184
ROWID 125, 127
runInstaller.................................... 43

S

security 66, 67, 137, 145, 155
segments.......................31, 33, 97, 98
Session-level waits 170
set serveroutput on 200
SGA 10, 13, 14, 15, 18, 20, 25, 29
sga_max_size 15

sga_target 15
shared pool.................. 15, 17, 18, 57
Shared SQL Area 18
shared_pool_size......................15, 17, 57
SHOW RECYCLEBIN 114
shutdown..22, 67, 70, 76, 77, 78, 91, 94, 178
SHUTDOWN 76
SHUTDOWN ABORT.................78
SID 51, 84, 168, 173
skewonly 121
SMON 24
snapshot too old............................98
sort_area_size 20
SPFILE.....28, 81, 82, 83, 84, 85, 86, 87, 177, 178, 181, 182, 183, 184
spfile.ora 86
spfileSID.ora 86
SQL 3, 18, 20, 110, 115, 135, 136, 137, 138, 145, 150, 154, 164, 168, 171, 186, 187, 188, 189, 191, 193, 195, 198, 201, 204, 205, 207
SQL*Plus62, 63, 65, 66, 67, 68, 186, 187, 188, 189, 192, 198, 200, 201, 202
Standard Edition 37
startup 28, 70, 72, 73, 74, 77, 78, 86, 87, 182
Structured Query Language........ 186
SWITCH LOGFILE.......................95
Symmetric Multiprocessing 39
Synonyms 152, 154
SYSAUX.............................. 31, 159
SYSDBA.................... 66, 67, 149
SYSOPER 66, 67, 149
SYSTEM ..31, 53, 97, 105, 114, 159, 163
System Global Area 13

T

tablespace31, 32, 33, 97, 98, 99, 100, 101, 102, 103, 106, 107, 112, 128, 129, 134, 146, 147, 159, 163, 164, 165
template................................50, 51, 60
temporary tablespace 102, 103
TEMPORARY TABLESPACE keyword 146
THEN clause 204, 205
tnsnames.ora.......................... 29, 187

U

undo_management...............................98
undo_retention 98
undo_tablespace 98
Unique constraints 141
Universal Installer........................ 42
UNIX 8, 43, 65, 83, 169, 196
user_ind_columns 134
user_indexes....................................134
user_tab_columns 114, 115
user_tables 114, 115, 160

V

v$ 79, 166
v$archived_log.....................................96
v$log 90, 96
v$log_history 96
v$parameter.................................85, 96
v$session 168, 169, 170
v$sql...169
v$system_event...............................171
v$system_wait_class....................171
varchar2.................. 106, 107, 139, 202
Views 79, 136, 137, 138, 166, 167, 168

W

WHERE clause 197
WHILE loop.........................206, 207
WITH ADMIN keyword 150
WITH ADMIN OPTION keyword
.... 150

WITH GRANT OPTION 152

X

x$ 167

About Steve Karam

Steve Karam is one of less than 20 DBA's worldwide to achieve the coveted *Oracle 10g Certified Master* status and he has been honored with the prestigious *Oracle ACE* designation. A former senior instructor for Oracle University, Steve has a proven track record in performance and troubleshooting on dozens of high profile Oracle systems, and complex Oracle 10g RAC environments.

Steve Karam is a senior Oracle consultant for Burleson Consulting (www.dba-oracle.com).

About Robert Freeman

 ***Robert G. Freeman*** is one of the most famous Oracle experts and author of eight popular Oracle books, including Oracle9i RMAN Backup & Recovery and the bestselling Oracle9i and Oracle10g New Features book. Robert is expert in UNIX and Oracle RAC and specializes in Oracle backup & recovery and performance tuning for complex databases.

Robert Freeman serves as a senior Oracle consultant for Burleson Consulting (www.dba-oracle.com).

About Mike Reed

When he first started drawing, Mike Reed drew just to amuse himself. It wasn't long though, before he knew he wanted to be an artist. Today he does illustrations for children's books, magazines, catalogs, and ads.

He also teaches illustration at the College of Visual Art in St. Paul, Minnesota. Mike Reed says, "Making pictures is like acting — you can paint yourself into the action." He often paints on the computer, but he also draws in pen and ink and paints in acrylics. He feels that learning to draw well is the key to being a successful artist.

Mike is regarded as one of the nation's premier illustrators and is the creator of the popular "Flame Warriors" illustrations at www.flamewarriors.com, a website devoted to Internet insults. "To enter his Flame Warriors site is sort of like entering a hellish Sesame Street populated by Oscar the Grouch and 83 of his relatives." – Los Angeles Times.
(http://redwing.hutman.net/%7Emreed/warriorshtm/lat.htm)

Mike Reed has always enjoyed reading. As a young child, he liked the Dr. Seuss books. Later, he started reading biographies and war stories. One reason why he feels lucky to be an illustrator is because he can listen to books on tape while he works. Mike is available to provide custom illustrations for all manner of publications at reasonable prices. Mike can be reached at www.mikereedillustration.com.

Free!
Oracle 10g Senior DBA Reference Poster

This 24 x 36 inch quick reference includes the important data columns and relationships between the DBA views, allowing you to quickly write complex data dictionary queries.

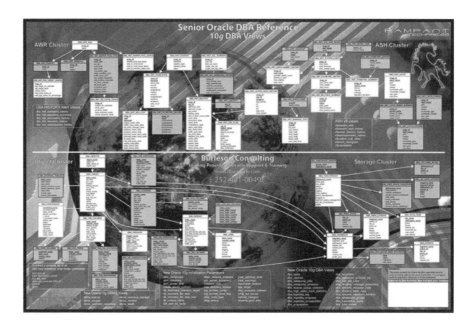

This comprehensive data dictionary reference contains the most important columns from the most important Oracle10g DBA views. Especially useful are the Automated Workload Repository (AWR) and Active Session History (ASH) DBA views.

WARNING - This poster is not suitable for beginners. It is designed for senior Oracle DBAs and requires knowledge of Oracle data dictionary internal structures. You can get your poster at this URL:

www.rampant.cc/poster.htm

Easy Oracle PL/SQL Programming

By John Garmany

Written by a distinguished graduate of West Point, Garmany leverages his 20+ years of experience into an indispensable guide for any Oracle professional who must quickly implement Oracle reporting.

A noted instructor, author, and lecturer, John Garmany leverages his ability to explain complex issues in Plain English into a one-of-a-kind book. Intended for anyone who needs to extract Oracle data and format reports, John reveals the secrets of quickly and easily producing stunning reports from Oracle.

Easy Oracle PL/SQL provides you with the tools you need to create, debug, and execute PL/SQL code. The example driven methodology will have you coding basic PL/SQL blocks by the end of the first chapter. Each chapter will build on previous concepts, introducing you to increasingly more complex PL/SQL coding, while always focusing on readability and manageability. Each concept is introduced using multiple examples and each chapter has exercises to test your knowledge. With Easy Oracle PL/SQL you will be able to put the incredible power of the Oracle Database to use with your application.

www.rampant.cc

Oracle PL/SQL Tuning

By Dr. Timothy Hall

Oracle experts know that PL/SQL tuning makes a huge difference in execution speed. As one of the world's most popular and respected experts, Dr. Tim Hall shares his secrets for tuning Oracle PL/SQL.

This indispensable book shows how to hypercharge Oracle applications gaining as much as 30x improvement in execution speed using under-documented code tricks. Packed with working examples, learn how to re-write SQL into PL./SQL and how to use advanced Oracle bulk array processing techniques to achieve super high performance. You can save your company millions of dollars in hardware costs by making your applications run at peak efficiency.

Targeted at the Senior Oracle DBA and developer, this advanced book illustrates powerful techniques that can make PL/SQL run faster than ever before. This book is not for beginners and should only be purchased by seasoned Oracle professionals who must turbo charge their applications. Your time savings from a single script is worth the price of this great book.

www.rampant.cc

Oracle Tuning: The Definitive Reference

Oracle 10g has become the most complex database ever created and Oracle tuning has become increasingly complex. This book provides a complete step-by-step approach for holistic Oracle tuning and it is the accumulated knowledge from tuning thousands of Oracle databases.

This is not a book for beginners. Targeted at the senior Oracle DBA, this book dives deep into the internals of the v$ views, the AWR table structures and the new DBA history views. Packed with ready-to-run scripts, you can quickly monitor and identify the most challenging performance issues.

Don't be left behind. Learn Oracle Tuning from the top experts!

www.rampant.cc